Diving In – An Incident Responder's Journey

A Guide for Executives, Lawyers, Insurance Professionals, and Audiences Eager to Learn

Devon Ackerman

"Diving In"

Copyright © 2023 by Devon Ackerman. All rights reserved.

No portion of this book may be reproduced in any form without written permission from the publisher or author, except as permitted by U.S. copyright law.

This publication is designed to provide accurate and authoritative information in regard to the subject matter covered. It is sold with the understanding that neither the author nor the publisher is engaged in rendering legal, investment, or accounting services. While the publisher and author have used their best efforts in preparing this book, they make no representations or warranties with respect to the accuracy or completeness of the contents of this book and specifically disclaim any implied warranties of merchantability or fitness for a particular purpose. No warranty may be created or extended by sales representatives or written sales materials. The advice and strategies contained herein may not be suitable for your situation. You should consult with a professional when appropriate. Neither the publisher nor the author shall be liable for any loss of profit or any other commercial damages, including but not limited to special, incidental, consequential, personal, or other damages.

Book Cover Design, Illustrations & Included Art by Devon Ackerman

First Edition 2023 v1.1

ISBN: 9798852408020

Library of Congress Control Number: 2023913223

Forward

Parts of this book will be out-of-date by the time you read it. Authoring moment-in-time snapshots of an ever-evolving digital world has unavoidable challenges, especially in print. This speed of evolution is one reason blogs and social media are so popular within the online communities of #InfoSec, #CyberSecurity, Digital Forensics and Incident Response (#DFIR), etc. As I was writing this book, working through the re-edits, re-imagining certain chapters with editors and feedback from professional and legal colleagues, I would find new information and have to update bookmarks and reference links due to new findings, events, and developments. By the time you read this, it is quite possible that certain citation and reference links will be dead and an online search for context may be necessary. Trying to write a single source of truth to address all of the topics that I envisioned covering in this book would have been a herculean task that would likely never have come to fruition or a proper book ending. Rather, I chose to write this book to provide you an educational and insightful overview to the world of Digital Forensics and Incident Response, intertwining learned moments from my experiences, career to present, investigations, discussions with industry peers, and my own research. I hope you learn something helpful within the chapters and pages of this book.

I carefully considered what topics to cover in this book, with an eye to **legal professionals** looking to more fully understand Digital Forensics; for **corporate executives** looking to explore key concepts, details, and follow-on considerations surrounding the world of Incident Response; and also for professionals involved in the world of **cyber insurance on the carrier and broker** sides looking to delve into why threat actors do what they do and how to become more educated around the many facets of data breaches that every day affect customers of all sizes. I have spent significant time filling these chapters for anyone wanting to learn, gain perspective, and enrich their viewpoints, to include my professional colleagues across geographies, cultures, enterprises, and governments.

For up-to-date information, you can find me on:

- **aboutdfir**.com
- twitter.com/**aboutdfir**
- linkedin.com/in/**devonackerman**
- kroll.com/en/our-team/**devon-ackerman**

Acknowledgements

This book is dedicated to the countless people who have contributed to my life's path, personally and professionally with everlasting thanks to my mother, "Debbie" Ackerman, whose memory lives on in my oldest daughter's middle name and in honor of her legacy of the tremendous impact she left upon those she called *"her loved ones."* Without her wanting the best for her son and looking for something new and upcoming and finding it randomly in a magazine article about Digital Forensics nearly twenty-five years prior to me sitting down to write this book, it is quite likely that my life choices would have led me in a different direction, one nowhere near as rewarding as the journey on which I currently find myself. My wife, my children, my family – thank you for the support over the many years of long days, business travel and pursuit of *"learning a thing or two about a thing or two."*

This book would also not be possible without the insights, input, feedback, editing, and encouragement of my professional colleagues, close friends, and immediate family who support me every day, every week. A special thank you to the editors, best friends, content reviewers and supporters who contributed their time: *Anna Johnson, Donna Correll, Scott Downie, Chris Ballod, Ben Demonte, Jason Smolanoff, Jack Bennett, Greg Johnson, Dan Cox, Harry Landis, Gibson Grose, Ron Rader, Hannah Danziger, Tony Knutson, David Sherman, Aleks Vold, and countless others.* Thank you each and all - We learn, teach, adapt, and love what we do.

```
00100010 01001110 01100101 01110110 01100101 01110010 00100000 01110011 01110100
01101111 01110000 00100000 01100101 01111000 01110000 01101100 01101111 01110010
01101001 01101110 01100111 00101100 00100000 01101110 01100101 01110110 01100101
01110010 00100000 01110011 01110100 01101111 01110000 00100000 01101100 01100101
01100001 01110010 01101110 01101001 01101110 01100111 00101110 00100010
```

TABLE OF CONTENTS

Chapter 1 - State of Modern Investigative Digital Forensics 10
    Data Is Everywhere, But Not Secure As You Might Think 12
    Internet Identity Fusing (IIF) 15
    How DFIR Protects and Helps Victims of Data Security Incidents 19
    Kroll DFIR Engagement Lifecycle 22
        Stage 0 and 1 - Scoping & Contracting 23
        Stage 2 - Kickoff 24
        Stage 3 and 4 - Triage and Containment 25
        Stage 5 and 6 - Interval Updates and Final Reporting 27
        Additional Services 28

Chapter 2 - Challenges & Considerations 30
    Beyond Tools – DFIR Requires Multidisciplined Experts 33
    Legal Aspects to Consider 37
    Anti-Forensics 38

Chapter 3 - Principles & Artifacts 47
    Locard's Exchange Principle 48
    Forensics Artifacts Overview 50
        File System Basics 51
        Web Browser Basics 59
        Browsing History 60
        Cookies 62
        Cache Files 64
        Download History 67
        Web Form Data and Saved Passwords 69
        Local Storage and IndexedDB 71
        Extension Data 74
        Browser Configuration Files 76

Registry Basics 77

Windows Event Log Basics 80

Event Tracing for Windows Basics 83

Prefetch Basics 86

Shellbag Basics 88

Chapter 4 - Causality & Ethics 94

The Relationship Between Cause and Effect 94

Ethical Handling of Original Evidence 96

Understanding and Interpreting Forensic Artifacts 98

Neutrality and Fact-Based Analysis 99

User Causality Determined from Digital Evidence 101

Chapter 5 - The Kroll Intrusion Lifecycle™ 102

The Constancy of the Criminal Mindset 105

The Kroll Intrusion Lifecycle™ - Stage by Stage 109

Stage 0 - External Victim Scouting 110

Stage 1 - Initial Exploit/Actor Foothold 112

Stage 2 - Internal Victim Scouting 113

Stage 3 - Toolkit Deployment 115

Stage 4 - Escalation 117

Stage 5 - Lateral Movement/Reconnaissance 118

Stage 6 - Execution of Mission 119

Chapter 6 - The Trickle Down Effect 120

Studying APT Tactics and Techniques 121

Adopting Similar Tools and Infrastructure 124

But Why Do They Do It? 125

Blurring Lines Between APT & Organized Criminal Groups 129

Turla 130

Notable Hacking & Big Game Hunting Stories 133

Lazarus Group 136

Notable Hacking & Big Game Hunting Stories 140

Clop 143

Notable Hacking & Big Game Hunting Stories 145

Chapter 7 - The Castle Doctrine 147

Defense in Depth: From Moats to Firewalls 152

Segmentation and Access Control: From Portcullises to VLANs 153

Monitoring and Alerting: From Watchtowers to SIEM Systems 154

Defending the Endpoint: Armored Guards to EDR Solutions 156

Chapter 8 - Incident Response Planning & Tabletop Exercises 158

Risk Assessment and Analysis 159

Incident Response Plan Development 160

Incident Response Plan Review and Enhancement 161

Tabletop Exercises and Simulations 162

Chapter 9 - Criminal Groups & Their Methods 164

Financially Motivated Groups 165

State-Sponsored Groups 167

Hacktivist Groups 177

Laundering Money via Crypto 182

The Digital Frontier – North Korea's Crypto Heists 185

Custom Malware Development 188

Polymorphic Malware 190

Malware as a Service (MaaS) 193

Research and Development 195

Initial Access Brokers (IAB) 201

Chapter 10 - Insider Threats 203

Chelsea Manning 205

Edward Snowden 206

Galen Marsh 207

Harold T. Martin 208

Jun Ying 209

Jack Teixeira 210

Analysis of Insider Threats: A Three-Category Perspective 211

    Malicious Insiders 212

    Negligent Insiders 214

    Accidental Insiders 216

Chapter 11 - Violence-as-a-Service 219

    Mexican Drug Cartels, US Military & Social Media Recruitment 222

    Hitmen, Crypto & Live Streaming 224

    Egregor Organized Crime Group & Triple Extortion 225

    Dark Overlord & Threats Against Children 226

    Bitcoin, the DarkWeb, & the Acid Attack 227

    Social Media & "Recruiting" for a School Mass Casualty 228

    Cocaine, Heroin & Millions in Cryptocurrency 229

    John Musbach, Murder-for-Hire & Crypto 230

    Swatting-as-a-Service (SaaS) 231

    Voice Cloning-as-a-Service (VCaaS) 234

Chapter 12 - Data Governance, Risk, and Compliance (GRC) Meet in #DFIR 239

    Data Security Controls 241

    Avoiding Blind Reliance on Cloud Service Providers 242

    Investing in Your Team 243

    Collaboration with Legal Teams 244

    Digital Forensics and GRC Teams in Harmony 245

Chapter 13 - "EDR, MDR & XDR, oh my!" 246

    Endpoint Detection and Response (EDR) 247

    Managed Detection and Response (MDR) 249

    Extended Detection and Response (XDR) 251

About the Author 253

Life and Pivotal Curveballs...255

AboutDFIR.com & Giving Back 259

54 68 65 72 65 20 61 72 65 20 6F 6E 6C 79 20 74 77 6F 20 68 61 72 64 20 74 68 69 6E 67 73
20 69 6E 20 63 6F 6D 70 75 74 65 72 20 73 63 69 65 6E 63 65 20 20 13 20 63 61 63 68 65 20
69 6E 76 61 6C 69 64 61 74 69 6F 6E 2C 20 6E 61 6D 69 6E 67 20 74 68 69 6E 67 73 20 61
6E 64 20 6F 66 66 2D 62 79 2D 6F 6E 65 20 65 72 72 6F 72 73 2E

CHAPTER 1 - STATE OF MODERN INVESTIGATIVE DIGITAL FORENSICS

Digital Forensics and Incident Response (DFIR) are two essential areas of investigative and reactive cybersecurity that aim to protect individuals, governments, and organizations of all sizes and complexity from ever-present, ever-evolving cyber threats. Legal counsel and cyber insurance carriers are often called upon by their clients to help start and navigate the Digital Forensics and Incident Response process.

Digital Forensic science, commonly referred to as digital or computer forensics, is the branch of forensic science that deals with the collection, analysis, and preservation of digital data — evidence of something that has occurred. It involves the investigative use of specialized tools and techniques to defensibly extract and analyze data from a ubiquitous and continually growing array of computers, tablets, servers, smartphones, smartwatches, network devices, Internet of Things (IOT),[1] etc. If it powers on and stores data, it can be analyzed.

In the context of cybersecurity, Digital Forensics is often used to investigate incidents such as ransomware events, network intrusions, insider threats, malware, intellectual property theft, cyber espionage, and cyber terrorism. By analyzing the digital evidence left behind, investigators can determine causes of incidents and gather evidence for legal action.

Incident Response is essentially the steps taken to address, contain, and minimize the impact of a cyberattack and prevent further damage. This process involves a range of activities, including identifying the scope of the incident, containing the attack, collecting evidence, analyzing the reach of the incident, and restoring affected systems and data. It requires a coordinated effort by a team of experts, including IT professionals, cybersecurity and Digital Forensics experts, and legal professionals.

---

[1] The Internet of Things (IoT) refers to a network of physical devices, vehicles, home appliances, and other objects that are embedded with sensors, software, and connectivity to allow them to exchange data and interact with other devices or systems over the internet. IoT enables devices to collect, analyze, and share data in real-time, which can be used to improve efficiency, productivity, and decision making in a variety of industries. IoT also poses significant security and privacy risks, as many devices lack adequate security measures and are vulnerable to cyberattacks, scriptable exploitation, or unauthorized access.

DATA IS EVERYWHERE, BUT NOT SECURE AS YOU MIGHT THINK

When we refer to *"evidence"* in the context of Digital Forensics, we are ultimately talking about data, and in today's modern world it is simply everywhere; from the computer on your desk to the cell phone in your pocket; from the smart devices in your home to the data you do not even realize is saved in the cloud on some company's own servers. What many people do not realize is how little control they individually have over much of their *"personal"* data, and all of the places its stored. For example, you might say that your personal computer, cell phone, and even social media interactions are all #things that you control, and you can just delete whenever you want to, because the device is in your hands, right?

But what about the data you provide to websites when you create an account? That data must be secure because they let you set a

Multifactor authentication (MFA) is a security measure that requires users to provide more than one form of authentication to access a system or application. This typically involves combining something the user knows, such as a password or PIN, with something the user has, such as a security token or smartphone, or something the user is, such as a fingerprint or facial recognition. In corporate login security, MFA provides an additional layer of protection against unauthorized access, especially in cases where passwords may be compromised or stolen. MFA can be implemented through a variety of methods, including SMS codes, mobile apps, smart cards, and biometric authentication, among others. By requiring multiple factors of authentication beyond a simple username and password prompt, MFA can raise the defenses of a login and user authentication process.

Diving In – An Incident Responder's Journey

password, have HTTPS[2], and offer multi-factor authentication (MFA) sign-in options, right?

What about your employer's network, where they store their backups, how they allow contractors and third parties access, and how they integrate cloud-connected single sign-on (SSO)[3] solutions?

How about the content you send in that free email account you have? Ever wondered why its offered for free and read the End User License Agreement (EULA)?

What about your doctor's office[4] and your family's healthcare network; they store and maintain all of your personally identifiable Information (PI/PII)

---

[2] Hypertext Transfer Protocol Secure (HTTPS) is a protocol used for secure communication over the internet. It is an extension of the standard HTTP protocol, which is used for transmitting data between a web browser and a web server. HTTPS employs a combination of Transport Layer Security (TLS) or Secure Sockets Layer (SSL) encryption and HTTP to provide a secure and encrypted connection between the user's browser and the server. This encryption ensures that any data transmitted between the two is protected from interception, tampering, or eavesdropping by third parties. HTTPS is commonly used for online transactions, such as online banking, e-commerce, and other activities that require secure communication over the internet.

[3] Single sign-on (SSO) is a method of access control that allows a user to authenticate once and gain access to multiple applications and systems without having to re-authenticate for each one. In corporate login security, SSO can simplify the login process for employees by providing a centralized authentication mechanism for all of the company's systems and applications, while also reducing the risk of password-related security breaches. SSO is commonly implemented through the use of identity and access management (IAM) systems, which provide a secure and efficient way to manage user authentication and access to corporate and network accessible resources.

[4] Hackers are now notoriously attacking healthcare networks due to the target-rich environments, smaller IT security budgets, and pressure that they can apply to victims to pay an extortion demand. See "Cyber Threat Intelligence Series: A Lens on the Healthcare Sector," Laurie Iacono and George Glass, Kroll, December 2022, www.kroll.com/en/insights/publications/cyber/cyber-threat-intelligence-healthcare-sector.

and protected health information (PHI) on HIPAA [5] compliant databases with *"military grade encryption,"* right? But about the insider threat aspect that already had authorized access to your data?

As I hope you'll learn from the following chapters, the data we rely upon for our personal and professional lives is stored in a myriad of ways and every network is a battleground between those protecting it and those looking to compromise it. Between those looking to "raise the defenses" and those looking to counter those defenses.

The National Institute of Standards and Technology (NIST) and the International Organization for Standardization (ISO) are two organizations that develop and publish technical standards and guidelines for a wide range of industries, including information technology, cybersecurity, and data privacy. NIST is a non-regulatory agency of the United States Department of Commerce that provides standards, guidelines, and best practices to help organizations manage and secure their information systems and data. ISO, on the other hand, is an independent, non-governmental organization that develops and publishes standards for various industries worldwide, including cybersecurity and privacy. The NIST Cybersecurity Framework and the ISO/IEC 27001 standard are two widely recognized and adopted frameworks for managing cybersecurity risk and protecting sensitive data. These standards provide a set of guidelines and best practices for organizations to follow in order to identify, assess, and mitigate cyber risks and protect their information assets.

---

[5] The Health Insurance Portability and Accountability Act of 1996 (HIPAA) is a United States federal law that required the creation of national standards to protect sensitive patient health information (PHI) from being disclosed without the patient's consent or knowledge. See "Health Insurance Portability and Accountability Act of 1996 (HIPAA)", www.cdc.gov/phlp/publications/topic/hipaa.html.

INTERNET IDENTITY FUSING (IIF)

All of the information flying around the internet that is digitally collected, stored, transmitted, and aggregated can be combined over time to identify and profile you. This is regularly referred to as *"digital fingerprinting,"* and even I often refer to the *"digital fingerprints or footprints"* of threat actors in my talks. All of that data, its bits and pieces, actually serves as the foundation for what I believe is the future organized crime groups having the technical data and the volume of data and reach to begin targeting individuals and organizations with scalpel-like specificity. I developed a model that I am introducing for the first time in this book — **Internet Identity Fusing (IIF)** — that reflects what I have witnessed being leveraged by threat actors, governments, criminals, and beyond to uniquely identify people, persons, and places across the internet.

What is IIF? I propose that threat actors are now, and will more so in the future, fuse together proactive research and data elements derived from disparate data breaches, open-source intelligence (OSINT), and closed sources (e.g., dark web, deep net, paid intelligence services), all in order to more strategically and tactically identify, target, and compromise not just exploitable systems, but the human behind the keyboard. After all, the weakest link in any network is the human element.[6]

---

[6] According to Verizon's 2023 Data Breach Investigations Report, *"74% of breaches involved the human element"*, i.e., people being taken in by social engineering or just making mistakes. Interestingly, Verizon noted that half of social engineering attempts involved *"pretexting"*, which doubled from the prior year. Pretexting is when actors come up with a convincing story (i.e., pretext) that draws on a trusted relationship (i.e., colleague or vendor the victim often works with and knows) in order to influence and manipulate action by the victim. www.verizon.com/business/resources/reports/dbir/

In my mind, IIF is the ultimate modern exploit and evolution of focus for threat actors. It is not a moment-in-time remote code execution (RCE) or tracked vulnerability (CVE) flavor of the day exploit that you just read about on your favorite security blog[7]. These inevitably have a limited lifecycles, from research and development (R&D) to active exploitation to detection to patching to go-forward reduced usefulness.

No, I propose that IIF is actually more of a tactical targeting of the unpatchable problem — humans.

CVE stands for Common Vulnerabilities and Exposures. It is a unique identifier assigned to a specific security vulnerability in software or hardware products. The CVE system provides a standardized method for identifying and tracking vulnerabilities and exposures across different platforms and products. Think of it as a code or reference number used by security professionals and software vendors to refer to specific vulnerabilities in a way that is easy to understand and share.

Humans are constantly interacting and interfacing, directly and indirectly, with digital data, systems, and varied technologies. IIF allows this and the next generation of cybercriminals to more strategically target and attack with increased precision. Not just by knowing who you are by an account name, but who you are behind the name, behind the proverbial keyboard, further removing anonymity due to aggregation of data elements from hundreds of sources. The websites you routinely visit[8], your password sequencing over time, your email addresses, your social media footprint, prior breaches of your private and personal information — all of this in totality is your digital

---

[7] I have heard internet rumors that www.AboutDFIR.com is a great resource.
[8] For example, there are lists of data breaches showing your account information, like your email addresses, across dozens or even hundreds of breached sites. In aggregate, this allows for profiling in and of itself.

self, resolved from disparate systems, websites, cloud environments, and beyond.

- What you do, what you have done, what you are planning to do in the future combined with where you travel, the accounts you create to access content, the passwords you choose, etc. What happens when your information undergoes a data breach and control over that data is lost — obtained by an unauthorized third party?
- What happens when fragments of who you are continue to be intercepted, leaked, and aggregated across multiple data breaches across multiple providers, websites, and *"trusted"*[9] third parties? A username here, a password there, a real birthdate here and a real photo there — suddenly merged and combined to create an accurate profile and timeline of your digital life, bleeding through and revealing your personal, real life.
- What possibilities exist when the realm of cyber crosses into the physical and the amorphous, anonymous threat actor sitting in a distant country sends you flowers and a card to your home address encouraging you to pay a ransom demand *"or else"* — leveraging information from your employer's network intrusion and a combination of internet research and state and county register-of-deeds lookup to find your publicly available tax records and home address. It's happened. I have worked these matters and have counseled clients on the response to these unnerving situations.

What could happen is that threat actors start taking advantage of your breached data to analyze and interpret your past choices to project or anticipate your future choices. I posit that IIF will allow threat actors to

---

[9] Irony intentional.

evolve beyond opportunistic and broad swatch targeting to expert and strategic targeting with higher rates of success. The *"Trickle Down Effect"* that you will read about further in this book will delve deeper into this premise as well as how it fits in the intrusion lifecycle[10] and the mindset of organized crime groups, advanced persistent threat groups, and lone wolves.

---

[10] Chapter 4

HOW DFIR PROTECTS AND HELPS VICTIMS OF DATA SECURITY INCIDENTS

So why does this all matter and what does it really mean? Because that is where my world of Digital Forensics and Incident Response can play a pivotal role in helping potential and actual victims. The investigations and engagements that I have been involved in for nearly twenty years now have shaped and aided in determining the root cause of how a cyber incident affects data about people, about you.

As of the writing of this book, the latest statistics created an urgent narrative around the need to address the increasing and continuous threat of cyberattacks upon personal data and organization's networks.

In 2022, IBM Security reported costs associated with data breaches averaged $4.35 million, up from $4.24 million and $3.86 million in 2021 and 2020, respectively.[11]

In 2021, Kroll, VMWare Carbon Black, and Red Canary surveyed 500 security and legal leaders that discovered *"93 percent of large organizations have suffered at least one*

The 2022 Internet Crime Report published by FBI's Internet Crime Complaint Center (IC3) showed the Bureau received 800,944 complaints that resulted in losses of $10.3 billion.

Investment fraud complaints produced the greatest losses at $3.3 billion - crypto-currency investment scams accounted for $2.57 billion of those losses.

Business email compromise (BEC) complaints resulted in losses of $2.74 billion.

In 2022 and 2023, BECs were consistently in the top 3 most commonly investigative case opening type by my global IR teams.

---

[11] IBM. (2023). The Future of Quantum Computing. IBM. www.ibm.com/downloads/cas/3R8N1DZJ

incident that led to a compromise of data over the past 12 months. And when a cyberattack occurs, 92 percent said they are not completely confident in their ability to identify the root cause."[12]

In all these cases, it is important to remember that costs and estimations are based on reported breaches, and these are likely just a fraction of the cybercrimes that occur. On March 29, 2022, Bryan A. Vorndran, Assistant Director of FBI Cyber Division, minced no words when he testified before the Committee on Judiciary, United States House of Representatives[13]: *"We have the strategy to act against our cyber adversaries, we can provide significant value, and we have shown we can be successful. But none of that matters, and we will not continue our success if we don't know about suspicious activity or that a compromise has occurred...We know victims of cyber intrusions, particularly large enterprises, risk negative publicity if they disclose being impacted by cybercrime, so many incidents are often addressed by the victim directly and are never reported to the public or law enforcement."*

Together, Digital Forensics and Incident Response work hand in hand to provide a comprehensive approach to managing cyber incidents. Digital Forensics provides the evidence needed to support an Incident Response investigation, while Incident Response provides the necessary measures to contain and mitigate the effects of a cyber incident and restore systems to normal operation. With the increasing sophistication of cyber threats, organizations must be prepared to respond quickly and effectively to mitigate the impact of an attack. Further, cybersecurity is not a one-and-done compliance checkbox as it is often looked at with a budget first to be trimmed

---

[12] Kroll. Future CIO Report: Cyber Incident Response Remains a Challenge. www.kroll.com/en/insights/publications/cyber/future-cio-report-cyber-incident-response

[13] "America Under Cyber Siege: Preventing and Responding to Ransomware Attacks: Hearing Before the S. Comm. on the Judiciary, 117th Cong. (July 27, 2021), statement of Bryan A. Vorndran, Assistant Director of FBI Cyber Division", https://docs.house.gov/meetings/JU/JU00/20220329/114533/HHRG-117-JU00-Wstate-VorndranB-20220329.pdf

by executives, and a fiscal analysis conducted through the lends of *"return on investment,"* it is a continuous journey of investment, testing, improvement, and training interwoven through the fabric of *"trust, but verify."*

Every day in the world of cyber security, exploits are being released into the wild; every day devices and software have new patches to close security vulnerabilities; every day employees are coming and going between companies leaving lists of security tasks incomplete. The problem is not an insurmountable one, but it is also not an trivial one to manage either without properly scaled budgets, teams, and training. Tone at the top matters for organizations. When there is a focus on security with proper budget and proper relationship building with consultants who are experts in their fields to prepare for and respond to incidents, business interruption costs are reduced, business continuity during incidents is improved, and spoliation of necessary evidence necessary to properly scope risk is reduced. Take it from me, there are two categories of clients that I work with every day; those that have experienced an incident and those that do not know they have experienced an incident.

KROLL DFIR ENGAGEMENT LIFECYCLE

Chances are, if you ask someone, *"What is an Incident Response engagement?"*, you will receive a generically high level response, especially if they themselves have been involved in an IR before. If their organization has created and regularly tested an incident response plan (IRP) with a tabletop exercise (TTX), then they will likely have a stronger feel for what to expect during the real thing, but outside of those that deal with IR day to day, knowing how an engagement begins, flows, and ends, and importantly, what they can ultimately expect, is likely of value from an educational perspective.

So, let us dive into a typical engagement (investigative) lifecycle from the beginning.

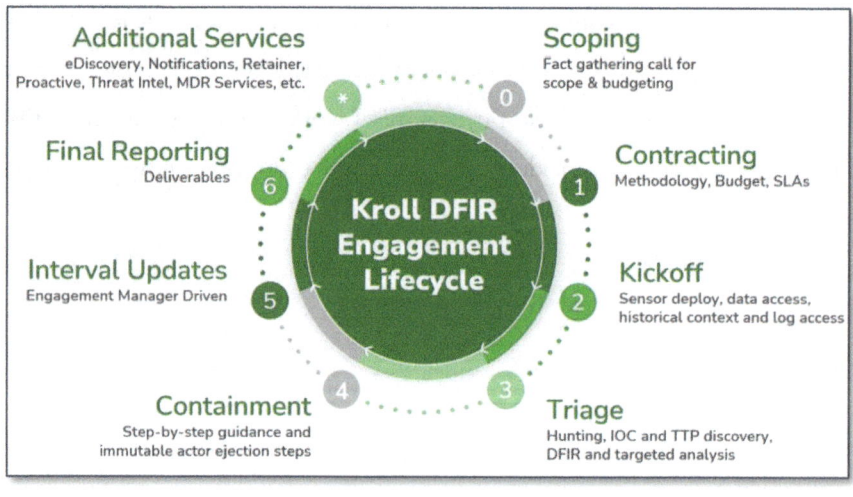

STAGE 0 AND 1 - SCOPING & CONTRACTING

When a victim of an incident has discovered that they are in need of outside DFIR expertise, typically a scoping call takes place between the victim of the incident (**client**), their chosen outside law firm (retaining **counsel** for purposes of providing legal guidance and providing attorney/client privilege over the investigative opinions, conclusions, and findings), and the **incident response consultant** (this is what I and my global IR teams do on a daily basis).

The purpose of the scoping call is to collect facts of what has occurred, to listen to the client explain what **has happened**, what they **know**, and what they **need**. My goal during the scoping is to listen and learn followed by capturing enough high level details about the layout of the client's networked environment to gain a baseline of knowledge to inform a proper scope and approach. My questions will often cover a range of topics. Examples include level of impact, number of endpoints (computers, servers, etc.), cloud systems, types of security software and scale of deployment, virtualization systems and types, state of backups for historical look-back or restoration capabilities, perimeter hardware (e.g., virtual private network (VPN), firewall, etc.), and more.

After the scoping call, contracts are created that follow a methodology and approach based on carefully considered next steps, to include an estimated budget. Contracts can cover a range of costs, tiers, and approaches for the client to decide on and choose which path they feel is right for them. This stage can involve the client's outside counsel for contract review as well as the client's cyber insurance carrier for budget review and approvals by the assigned claims manager.

STAGE 2 - KICKOFF

Kickoff coordination ideally occurs as soon as contracts are signed. Some typical kickoff activities can include recommending immediate containment steps; introducing assigned teams and the engagement manager ("EM" aka the point person of the engagement and conveyer of updates ideally as a singular voice throughout for consistency); and sharing of instructions for deployment of forensic tooling (Endpoint Detection and Response) and/or access to data and logging requests. The team assigned may be made up of analysts, forensic examiners, and operations or project managers, as well as specialist support teams as necessary and relevant. These specialists might consist of threat intelligence, litigation support, malware reverse engineers, data recovery, strategic and crisis communications, etc.

Email is popular for coordinating activities, but I have learned over the years that when initially stepping into a client's environment, it is like walking into a house for the first time with the lights off. Time is needed to explore, learn, and identify *"what is where"* in addition to ensuring that a threat actor is not still watching, observing, and learning what strategies the victim and their Incident Response consultant are going to choose. Just as DFIR practitioners learn from threat actors by the clues and evidence they leave behind, so, too, do threat actors want to learn how they are investigated. They do not want to be caught. They want intelligence to protect themselves as much as I want intelligence to chase, contain, and root them out. It is strongly encouraged, depending on the facts of the engagement and event in context, to not immediately trust internal chat communication platforms or email until access has been independently verified - *"Trust but verify"* and defensibly controlling the flow of information as much as being aware of your surroundings when walking into a strange house with the lights off for the first time.

STAGE 3 AND 4 - TRIAGE AND CONTAINMENT

Once access is obtained in some form or capacity, the Incident Response consultant needs to start threat hunting, to identify indicators of compromise (IOC) as well as tactics, techniques, and procedures (TTPs) of the threat actor in order to properly respond and react. Commonly, my teams are starting *"right-of-boom,"* meaning the incident has already occurred and we are entering the proverbial crime scene after the event has already taken place. This means that we are walking through **The Kroll Intrusion Lifecycle™** from end to beginning, more of which will be discussed thoroughly in Chapter 5.

Evidence will be pulled from key internal systems and logging platforms to begin forming an incident timeline of what occurred. At this point, the available evidence will look a lot like when someone has dumped out a puzzle on a living room table in front a large bay window with a view of a beautiful ocean beyond. All around, there are distractions, but you start looking for clues in the edges of the puzzle, the boundary lines, and once the corners are discovered, moving forward with assembling the final picture. So too do DFIR practitioners begin by connecting pieces of the forensic puzzle, working through recursive hunts, data collections, and analysis, until the relevant evidence has been exhausted and the assembled timeline resolves into a cohesive picture of what occurred historically – the finished, assembled puzzle. Sometimes those timelines can present startling revelations to clients, especially in instances where the intrusion started long before the client's view of what they believed occurred.

I had an investigation once where a client was implored by outside counsel to hire outside consultants to function as an *"independent, third party, verifier of fact"* not because the internal team's findings were untrusted, but for presenting to the client's third parties that they had *"nothing to hide, that their team and outside experts had reached independent, but matching conclusions.*" The Client, a prior victim to an intrusion and ransomware event, had restored their systems, had conducted an internal investigation with their team, and had drawn certain conclusions around data at risk and that no data exfiltration event had occurred. Ultimately, the client and outside counsel engaged my team and we worked through **The Kroll Intrusion Lifecycle™** in lockstep with them, transparently walking through the how, why, and where of our analysis and findings. It was during the evidence analysis stage that our team identified evidence that the threat actor had indeed exfiltrated data from the client's network, and that they had done so not over just the couple of weeks that the client assessed that they were in, but over the course of nearly five months across nearly seven different internal systems and via three separate data exfiltration methods. Our team discovered that the threat actor was able to stay under the client's radar for so long by leveraging not only authorized file transfer tooling that already existed within the client's network ("*living off the land*" approach), but also legacy email software that allowed for extremely normal-looking traffic carrying data out of the network through open, business approved ports. The threat actor did not need to bring in custom malware or new tooling that would have created louder signatures and potentially triggered security software alerts, they hid in the noise of the normal business operating profile of the enterprise.

In the end, we were able to overlay our investigative findings with the clients and show that both teams had conducted robust and detailed work. The approach that I leverage in walking through the **The Kroll Intrusion Lifecycle™** provides the context that executive teams are usually looking for as they are hungry to understand, "*what happened, how did it happen, why did happen, and how do we keep it from happening again*".

STAGE 5 AND 6 - INTERVAL UPDATES AND FINAL REPORTING

Throughout an investigation, the engagement manager is constantly being updated by the internal teams with new data points, findings, and the puzzle pieces that will eventually make up the final presentation. For interval updates, there are a range of presentation mediums, but what I have found works well is a combination of verbal discussion enhanced with a PowerPoint slide deck[14]. The slides follow a strict presentation of facts and visual timeline to paint the picture against **The Kroll Intrusion Lifecycle™** of what has been found up to that point in time in the investigation. Iterative updates fill in more of the blanks and answer more of the client's questions until the available evidence is exhausted and no further investigative leads are available or are relevant to pursue.

I have found that final, documented reporting is at the direction of counsel and/or the client. Sometimes a final report captured in long, narrative form, is not as relevant based upon the findings. There are occasions where an executive summary of findings may be all that is required in order to educate third parties or regulators, or even for the client's internal record-keeping. In any instance of reporting, I impress upon my teams as best practice that the forensic reporting must move through a **peer** review process that includes **technical** accuracy checks, **admin** review (consistent use of terminology and grammar checks), and **leadership** review (attention to detail, accuracy of story, and alignment of reporting against findings and asks from client and/or counsel). Then the reporting flows through counsel (when retained by client) for **legal** review and finally through client for **final** reviews before signing off and going *"pencils down."*

---

[14] Because everyone loves a good PowerPoint, right? Right?

ADDITIONAL SERVICES

Inevitably, no matter whether the investigation focused on a business email compromise, ransomware, intellectual property theft event, or something else, there should be findings and recommendations that result from the engagement. Sometimes, state and federal laws as well as regulatory guidance and policies drive the need for additional consultancy services, and other times, the education about the circumstances and facts uncovered about the incident drives a business need for additional services that had not been prior contemplated or budgeted for. Regardless of the motivators, a well-rounded Incident Response consultancy will have the ability to continue supporting the client forward beyond the immediate investigation. This can include any number of services, to include:

- Litigation support and **eDiscovery**-related data review[15]
- **Threat Intelligence** [16] to analyze and address post-incident exposure of organization's data, credentials, etc., on the dark web and social media
- Breach **notification**, call centers, and **monitoring**, to include credit and identify monitoring and identity theft restoration services[17]
- **Managed Detection and Response** (MDR) services for long-term endpoint detection [18] and proactive protection of assets and endpoints, to include email account monitoring[19]
- **Assessments** and testing services (e.g., penetration testing) for security gaps and assessing for application and cloud security gaps[20]

---

[15] www.kroll.com/en/services/cyber-risk/incident-response-litigation-support/phi-pii-identification
[16] www.kroll.com/en/services/cyber-risk/managed-security/cyberdetecter/cyberdetecter-darkweb
[17] www.kroll.com/en/services/cyber-risk/notification-monitoring
[18] www.kroll.com/en/services/cyber-risk/managed-security/kroll-responder
[19] www.kroll.com/en/services/cyber-risk/managed-security/kroll-responder/office-365
[20] www.kroll.com/en/services/cyber-risk/assessments-testing

- **Retainer** services allowing for a Master Services Agreement (MSA) to be pre-negotiated ahead of a need for services so that terms, conditions, and signatures are smooth and expedient[21]

---

[21] www.kroll.com/en/services/cyber-risk/incident-response-litigation-support/cyber-incident-response-retainer

CHAPTER 2 - CHALLENGES & CONSIDERATIONS

Digital Forensics has undergone a remarkable transformation over the past two plus decades. When Digital Forensics first emerged, it was characterized by manual hex-level interpretation of finite volumes of data, which necessitated a computer science-level understanding of digital storage. This was a time when Moore's law was unfolding before our eyes and technology was pushing development and release cycle improvements on a quarterly, if not monthly basis. As computing power grew, so too did the amount of digital information that was being generated and this exponential growth in data drove the need for increased storage. Economic laws governing supply and demand kicked in and we saw the emergence and evolution of storage media; floppy discs gave way to CDs which evolved to DVDs, Zip discs and thumb drives; physical storage eventually gave way to digital distribution, online cloud storage, and streaming over the internet. Computers that originally only featured volatile memory soon expanded to hard drives that grew in size from 5 megabytes (MB) that took four people to move back in 1956 [22] to thousands of petabytes in 2023 that fit in a single racks in a data center.

As software development became more complex, bandwidth connecting to/from the internet also matured, with dialup modems giving way to DSL, cable modems, fiber,

Moore's Law is a prediction made by Gordon Moore, one of the co-founders of Intel Corporation, in 1965. It states that the number of transistors that can be placed on a microchip doubles every 18-24 months, while the cost of the chip remains the same or decreases. The prediction has held true for several decades, with microchips becoming increasingly smaller, faster, and more powerful over time. This has led to significant advancements in computing power and has facilitated the development of new technologies, such as smartphones, personal computers, and the Internet of Things (IoT). Moore's Law has become a guiding principle for the technology industry, with many companies using it as a benchmark for the development of new products and technologies. However, as microchips have become smaller and more complex, it has become increasingly difficult to continue doubling the number of transistors on a chip every 18-24 months. Many experts predict that Moore's Law will eventually reach its limit, but new technologies, such as quantum computing, may provide alternatives to traditional microchips and continue the trend of ever-increasing computing power.

---

[22] "5 MB harddrive being shipped by IBM – 1956". Reddit online forum post. https://reddit.com/r/OldSchoolCool/comments/3l18hv/5_mb_harddrive_being_shipped_by_ibm_1956

and even satellite connections at our homes and offices. Despite this tremendous growth in digital information and storage capacity, humans still have a voracious appetite for consumption of digital information, even if they do not fully comprehend the underlying technology that makes it possible. Digital forensics has thus had to evolve to keep pace with these developments and has increasingly become a critical component of the broader cybersecurity and investigative landscapes.

SG93IGVhc3kgaXMgaXQgdG8gY291bnQgaW4gYmluYXJ5PyBJdHMgYXMgZWFzeSBh cyAwMSAxMCAxMS4=

BEYOND TOOLS – DFIR REQUIRES MULTIDISCIPLINED EXPERTS

Digital Forensics can be categorized into four main areas: **live** forensics (Incident Response), **static** forensics (dead box), **network** forensics (data-in-motion), and **cloud** forensics (hope and a prayer).

- **Live forensics** involves the analysis of running systems and the related telemetry encompassing system processes, program execution, etc.[23] Most traditionally executed with endpoint detection and response (EDR) sensor technologies.

- **Static forensics** involves the analysis of a system that has been shut down or captured as a snapshot of data in time, traditionally referred to as a forensic image. Commonly part of traditional forensics with systems that cannot be run in a live state, especially in a post-ransomware event where partial system encryption has occurred breaking the ability for the system to boot any longer.

- **Network forensics** involves the analysis of network traffic, data in motion, to identify communications between networked endpoints and passing through perimeter appliances. Commonly involving log acquisition and analysis as derived from firewalls, edge routers, VPN appliances, etc., not much unlike cloud forensics as its own category.

- **Cloud forensics** is an overly broad category and is arguably a combination of all three of the aforementioned in some form or another with a heavy focus on log-specific analysis. I noted *"hope and a prayer"* above and that is because Software as a Service (SaaS), Infrastructure as a Service (IaaS), and Platform as a Service (PaaS) consistently provide convoluted, varied, and non-standardized

---

[23] More in the final Chapter of this book focused on EDR concepts and considerations.

logging availability, not to mention logging settings defaulting to off or "*light*" detail modes. And all of this is in addition to licensing-level complexities that equally affect available logging and evidence accessibility when it's needed for investigations. Over the years of my investigative experience, I have found that all too many many cloud-based platforms default to hidden and undocumented settings.

This is arguably a step backwards for DFIR after years of documented and defensible process documentation. We as practitioners are now in a generation of investigations focused on layered and obfuscated software solutions outside of our tangible reach. Defensible data collection and investigations are frustrated by the removal of traditional hands-on forensic access. Beginning an investigation with the "*hope and a prayer*" that the needed evidence is turned on or *"available upon request"* is commonplace, but we know we equally need to be prepared to test, document, and research because the onus then falls on us as the investigators to provide meaning and context to the incident (causality) as well as overcome significant challenges to independently reproduce a threat actor's attack pattern within some cloud platforms when not all of the puzzle pieces are available to us.

Additionally, Digital Forensics typically involves four (4) key steps:

- **Acquisition** – Creating a forensically sound preservation of the data in question to save and analyze. Typically, forensics involves the creation of a **best evidence** copy and a **derivative evidence** copy — best evidence copy for storage and future validation checks and a derivative evidence copy to work with, i.e., for tool execution and processing.

- **Integrity** – Integrity (hashing[24]) checks and maintaining a chain-of-custody process to ensure defensibility and reproducibility of data without alteration, obliteration, or compromise.
- **Analysis** – Using specialized software tools, scripts, and techniques to extract relevant evidence from the digital media and applying expert knowledge, training, and experience to arrive at findings and conclusions.
- **Reporting** – Verbal and written presentation of the results of the forensic analysis in a defensible, factual, and technically accurate manner that is understandable to a broad range of listeners, both technical experts and laypersons.

DFIR experts use a variety of tools and techniques to extract and analyze digital evidence. We may use forensic imaging processes to create a bit-for-bit copy of original evidence, allowing for preservation without altering the original data. We leverage hash verification for addressing authenticity questions and we use triage approaches to expeditiously preserve ephemeral, ever-changing data as a moment-in-time snapshot and best evidence copies. Like any other tool development in modern history, the evolution of digital forensic software and hardware has been driven by a desire to refine and optimize analysis curves, automate repetitive tasks and attack the ever-

---

[24] Hashing in Digital Forensics is a process used to verify the integrity of data. It involves creating a unique identifier, known as a hash value or checksum, for a set of data, such as a file or a disk image. This hash value is generated using a specific algorithm, such as MD5 (Message Digest 5) or SHA (Secure Hash Algorithm). The key characteristic of a hash function is that it will always produce the same hash value when given the same input data. However, even a small change in the input data will result in a significantly different hash value.

evolving pattern of growing data sets in order to move through analysis of definable, structured data in reasonable time turnarounds.

In recent years, we have seen the scientific discipline of Digital Forensics increasingly commoditized, driven in large part by the need to categorize and enumerate larger and larger amounts (volume) of datasets into manageable categories. While automation has its place for repetitive processes, it can also be a bit of curse because as parts of my industry have swung towards automations and *"push button"* forensics, a portion of the forensics community has begun teetering on the edge of forgetting that possession of hands-on knowledge and proper understanding of causality [25] are the foundation of Digital Forensic Science – not that a tool *"did the work for you."*. The foundational knowledge to know how to ask oneself during an incident response such questions such as *"Why does this artifact relate to a user's action?"* and *"What does the forensic evidence tell us in the absence of specific artifacts?"* are key.

Forensic examiners must have a deep understanding of the principles and processes involved in Digital Forensics. They must be familiar with the underlying architecture of digital storage devices, logging, and why artifacts exist or are created the way they are.

---

[25] Discussed in greater depth and expanded upon in the next chapter.

LEGAL ASPECTS TO CONSIDER

Forensic examiners must be able to defensibly recover/extract relevant evidence, preserve it, and present findings in a manner that it can be legally used in the identification and attribution of cybercrime. This includes being able to articulate why and what digital evidence means in the context of its discovery as well as being able to remain objective, scientific, and non-biased. **Evidence is evidence, facts are facts.** In the context of digital forensic science, being non-biased refers to conducting investigations in an impartial and objective manner, without allowing personal beliefs, expectations, or preconceived notions to influence the process or outcomes of the investigation.

Objectively collect & analyze

The examiner should use standardized procedures and techniques to collect and analyze digital evidence, without selectively choosing or ignoring evidence based on personal bias.

Interpret findings impartially

The examiner should interpret the results of their analysis based on the evidence alone, not on what they expect or want the results to be.

Report accurately & honestly

The examiner should report their findings truthfully and accurately, including any limitations or uncertainties in the evidence or analysis.

Avoid conflicts of interest

The examiner should not have any personal or financial interests that could potentially influence their work.

ANTI-FORENSICS

Anti-forensics is a rapidly evolving field that presents a significant challenge to the world of Digital Forensics and Incident Response. At its core, anti-forensics refers to methods, tools, or techniques that obstruct, impede, or hinder the investigative and forensic science process. Steps taken to frustrate preservation, collection, and interpretation of evidence, thereby making the task of investigators more difficult and sometimes impossible, is the goal of anti-forensics. The concept of anti-forensics is not new. It has been a part of criminal activity for as long as forensics itself has existed. However, in the digital age, the scope and complexity of anti-forensic techniques have expanded dramatically.

I recall an investigation in which an organization that retained me for services had identified that they had become the victim of a data theft event. It was not until after my Incident Response teams had spent time investigating nearly 70 separate systems (and triaged nearly 13,000 systems at scale leveraging endpoint detection and response (EDR) sensor technology + Kroll Artifact Parser and Extractor (KAPE) [26] within the client's global enterprise), that we pieced together a nearly three-year-long threat actor monitoring campaign consistent with subtle data theft over time from nearly all aspects and departments of the enterprise – finance, human resources, research and development, code word software development programs, internal think tank projects, legal, copyright & trademark, and others. The threat actors had employed a range of anti-forensic techniques to cover their tracks and remain nearly invisible for those years, evading even evolving internal security software changes within those three years. Forensics and my

---

[26] Kroll Artifact Parser And Extractor (KAPE). www.kroll.com/en/services/cyber-risk/incident-response-litigation-support/kroll-artifact-parser-extractor-kape

team's assessment of key markers within the timeline we created indicated that the actors kept a continuous watch on the organization's internal procurement, contract review, and software purchasing processes to stay ahead of security vendor adoptions pre-deployment; in this way, they were able to alter their techniques and movement of their malware and beachhead systems to specifically avoid detection.

The threat actors also leveraged significant encryption to protect their malicious payloads, completely obfuscating their payloads, and even going so far as to log into the security solutions and whitelist their own malware so as to avoid alerting. My teams additionally found evidence of altered system logs and manipulated timestamps to create a false timeline of events. We even identified, contained, and removed two separate rootkits that we assessed were leveraged to both conceal and maintain persistence should other avenues of access be detected and contained.

In such an investigation, the Incident Response team faces an uphill battle from the beginning because the playing field of forensics changes with the sophistication of the threat actor's knowledge, skillset, and desire to remain hidden. The implications of these techniques extend beyond the immediate impact on the investigation. They can also undermine the legal process, as the lack of clear, reliable evidence can hinder prosecution efforts. In some scenarios, a lack of evidence and gaps in a reconstructed timeline leaves questions as to *"was something missed"* or *"what really happened during this period of unknown in which forensic evidence just does not exist?"*

At a high level, here are several key topics and areas of anti-forensics that you should be acquainted with.

- **Encryption** in its most basic explanation is a process of converting accessible (readable) data into something inaccessible without a decryption key or process. The forensic implications of encryption are significant. If an investigator encounters encrypted data during an investigation, they may be unable to access the information contained within without the appropriate decryption key. This can hinder the investigation process and potentially prevent access to crucial evidence. This is commonly the case during ransomware Incident Response investigations where key systems and data have been encrypted and analysis is stalled pending decryption or hopeful reliance on intact backups from a close enough timeframe to still be relevant. This is commonly the case during criminal investigations, such as with the well-documented case of the San Bernardino shooting in 2015, that my former organization, myself, and my colleagues were involved with, where the FBI faced technical and legal challenges in accessing data on the shooter's encrypted iPhone 5c running iOS 9.[27] This is also commonly run into during insider threat investigations in which stolen data is stored in encrypted

---

[27] Harwell, D. (2021, April 14). The FBI wanted to unlock the San Bernardino shooter's iPhone. It turned to a little-known Australian firm. The Washington Post. www.washingtonpost.com/technology/2021/04/14/azimuth-san-bernardino-apple-iphone-fbi

volumes or removable drives and the password is not voluntarily provided to investigators.

- **Obfuscation** involves making data, code, or processes difficult to understand. This technique can significantly hinder digital forensic investigations by making it challenging to analyze the data or code involved. For instance, malware authors often use obfuscation to mask and obfuscate the true purpose of their code, making it more difficult for security researchers and forensic investigators to understand functionality and origin without extensive time into reverse engineering.

- **False Flag** operations involve deliberate misdirection, typically through masquerading and mimicking tactics and techniques of another threat actor. This technique can mislead investigators about the source of an attack or unauthorized access. This is commonly the case with sophisticated government-

The Zeus Trojan, also known as Zbot, was a type of malware that used advanced obfuscation techniques to hide its true purpose and evade detection. This malware was designed to steal banking information through keystroke logging and form grabbing, and it was also used to install the CryptoLocker ransomware. The code of Zeus was heavily obfuscated and encrypted, making it challenging for reverse engineers to understand its functionality and origin. Further, Zeus had the ability to conceal its malicious code within large blocks of code that appeared legitimate, a technique known as "code blending" or "code mixing." This tactic is commonly used by malware authors to avoid detection by antivirus software and to make manual reverse engineering analysis more difficult.

sponsored advanced persistent threat (APT) groups who operate with government-backed intelligence collection directives. This was the suspected concept behind the 2018 Olympic Destroyer malware attack designed to disrupt the Winter Olympics in Pyeongchang, South Korea. During analysis, evidence seemed to point toward North Korea or China-based APT groups, but Incident Response and malware reverse engineers identified that while the code writers had carefully constructed the malware to include code snippets and clues that mimicked code popularly associated with the Lazarus Group[28, 29], evidence and deeper dives also led to a generally held assessment that steps had been taken to deliberately misdirect, even identifying *"…bits of malware code that linked Chinese-affiliated cyber espionage groups APT3 (Gothic Panda), APT10 (MenuPass Group), and APT12 (IXESHE)."* It was largely assessed that Lazarus Group's code snippets had been planted in a manner that were *"too obvious,"* almost as if the threat actors behind the malware's creation had deliberately wanted a range of nation finger-pointing in the wrong directions. Analysis led some researchers to suspect Russian-linked APT28 (Fancy Bear) threat group being behind the Olympic Destroyer malware,[30] but multiple vendors arrived at separate conclusions on source and genesis of the malware.

- **Onion routing** is a technique used for anonymous communication over a network, commonly the internet. The forensic implications of onion routing are significant because it can make it extremely difficult for investigators to accurately trace the true source of threat

---

[28] Kaspersky Lab. (2018). Olympic Destroyer: who hacked the Olympics? https://usa.kaspersky.com/blog/olympic-destroyer/14867/
[29] North Korean state-sponsored threat actor covered more thoroughly in Chapter 6.
[30] Axios. (2018, March 8). Report: Olympic Destroyer malware a false flag operation. www.axios.com/2018/03/08/olympic-destroyer

actors. The Onion Router (TOR) is a specific implementation of onion routing involving a network of servers that implement the onion routing protocol, allowing for obfuscated, anonymized network trafficking, and has been used in numerous cases to hide the identity of individuals involved in illegal activities, such as the infamous Silk Road marketplace.

- **Steganography** involves hiding data within other data. This technique can make it difficult for investigators to even realize that there is hidden data to be found in the first place. For example, an image file might contain a hidden message or file within its pixels. Unless investigators are aware of the possibility of steganography and have the tools to detect it, this hidden data might go unnoticed. This has been found in certain investigations that I have been involved with over the years and in sophisticated command-and-control malware implementations. The Vawatrak malware[31] was an example of this in which the malware leveraged steganography to hide IP addresses and web domains of its command-and-control channels in website favicon images, small images automatically downloaded by a web browser and usually displayed in the corner of a browser's window when on certain websites. This technique allowed the malware to communicate covertly and largely undetected until incident responders uncovered the technique.

---

[31] Pevný, T., Kopp, M., Kroustek, J., & Ker, A. D. (2016). Malicons: Detecting Payload in Favicons. https://ora.ox.ac.uk/objects/uuid:895a0272-412f-4a64-ba07-70c2c497dd88/

- **Rootkits** are a category of malicious software (malware) that is designed to hide its presence or the presence of other software on a computer. One example of a bootkit rootkit that was found in 2022 during Incident Response was CosmicStrand. It was designed to operate outside of the operating system layer of a computer and could survive a reboot of the computer system and a reload of the operating system (e.g., surviving a hard drive wiping, formatting, and complete software restore or reload). The rootkit was designed to infect vulnerable UEFI[32]

A bootkit is a type of rootkit that infects the Master Boot Record (MBR), Volume Boot Record (VBR), or Boot Configuration Data (BCD) of a computer. These areas are used to load the operating system when the computer is turned on, which means a bootkit can take control of the computer before the operating system even starts up. This gives the bootkit a high level of control over the system and makes it particularly difficult to detect and remove.

Like other rootkits, bootkits are designed to hide their presence and provide unauthorized access or control over a system. However, because they load before the operating system and can control how it starts up, they can effectively hide from antivirus software and other security tools that run within the operating system environment.

---

[32] Unified Extensible Firmware Interface (UEFI), is a type of software that helps your computer start up. You can think of it like a bridge that connects your computer's hardware and its operating system (like Windows or macOS) when you turn it on. Before your computer's operating system starts up, the UEFI software checks to make sure the computer's internal components (hardware) are working correctly. It is like an orchestra conductor

firmware versions of Gigabyte and Asus motherboards[33].

- **Changing timestamps (time stomping)** on files or within logs can mislead investigators about when certain events occurred. This can be used to mislead investigators, confuse timelines, or to hide the occurrence of certain activities. For instance, a threat actor might alter the timestamps on log entries to make it appear as though their activity occurred at a different time, potentially leading investigators on a false trail[34]. This is also more interesting than outright data destruction or deletion in that it takes time and experience to separate altered data from outright destroyed data.

- **Outright data destruction** or **secure file deletion** involves completely removing a file from a storage device. This can prevent investigators from recovering potentially important evidence. For example, an individual involved in illegal activities might use secure deletion tools to remove incriminating files from their computer before it can be seized for investigation. I had an investigation a few years ago of an insider threat that had taken deliberate actions before separating from their employer. In the weeks leading up to their sudden separation, they leveraged their placement and access to steal significant volumes of data from internal file and mail servers and then securely wiped their three physical office computers and their one virtual desktop instance before abruptly resigning and walking out the front door. When the company realized the steps that had

---

checking if all of the musicians are ready before the concert begins. If there is a problem, UEFI tries to fix it or lets the user know. Once everything is good to go, UEFI hands over control to the operating system, and a computer starts up as usual. UEFI is a modern replacement for Basic Input/Output System (BIOS) which had been around since the 1970s, designed for the original IBM PCs.

[33] Glazova, J. (2022, July 26). CosmicStrand: a UEFI rootkit. Kaspersky Lab. https://usa.kaspersky.com/blog/cosmicstrand-uefi-rootkit/26807/

[34] Kroll. Anti-Forensic Techniques – Timestomping. www.kroll.com/en/insights/publications/cyber/anti-forensic-tactics/anti-forensics-tactics-timestomping

been taken and had retained my team to investigate, large portions of original evidence had been deliberately destroyed and irrevocably lost as well as inadvertently "*stepped on*"[35] by the client's internal IT team who had tried to reconstruct what had happened. My team was still successful in creating derivative evidence-based timelines and evidence reconstruction from other systems within the network, to include a particularly useful data loss prevention (DLP) logging system that allowed for me to present back to the client a listing of files accessed and copied to and from the prior employee's system on specific dates and times. While the best evidence systems no longer existed due to the deliberate data destruction tactics, alternative analysis still led to a successful outcome that was ultimately referred to law enforcement.

---

[35] "*Let me be clear*" - it's generally not a good idea to reload an operating system over top of a freshly wiped hard drive in hopes of "*Getting it to boot…*"

CHAPTER 3 - PRINCIPLES & ARTIFACTS

I admit that I struggled a bit while authoring and conducting the research to fully build out this chapter. As an investigator, I find myself passionately diving into the deep technical end of certain topics and it was certainly humbling having editors redline this book at a herculean level to balance out my tangents.

My goal for this book is that you as a reader do not feel you need to have a degree in computer science or Digital Forensics to understand, appreciate, and learn something new. **This chapter dives a bit deeper into technical aspects of DFIR than other parts of this book, but it is for a specific reason. I know that when people are not familiar with terms commonly used in DFIR conversation, they find it hard to follow along on update calls or connect the dots when reading the final IR report.** The material I have covered in the following sections seeks to demystify common technical terms and concepts and help you walk away with contextual or reference knowledge and analogies for the next time you are listening or helping your clients understand what happened in their incident.

LOCARD'S EXCHANGE PRINCIPLE

Locard's Exchange Principle is a fundamental concept in traditional forensic science, which posits that *"every contact leaves a trace."* In other words, any interaction between an individual and their environment will result in the transfer of physical evidence that can serve as a clue in a forensic investigation. This principle is often associated with the idea of fingerprints, which are unique to each individual and can provide evidence of their presence at a crime scene. It is a principle that I propose underscores **Internet Identity Fusing** as discussed earlier in Chapter 1. Other examples of physical evidence include DNA, tool marks, chemical elements, clothing fibers, and others.

__Dr. Edmond Locard__ was a French criminologist often referred to as the "Sherlock Holmes of France." Born in 1877, he made significant contributions to the field of forensic science during the early 20th century. In 1910, he established the world's first police laboratory in Lyon, France, which became a model for modern forensic labs around the world.

In Digital Forensics, Locard's Exchange Principle is equally applicable, albeit in a digital context. The principle recognizes that actions, interactions, and operations in an environment leave behind evidence of reactions that can serve as evidence in a forensic investigation — if one knows where to look, how to collect without compromising, and how to defensibly interpret and articulate meaning.

Just like the real world, crime scenes are affected by time, passersby, investigators, forensic analysts, etc. So too is the digital world, but unlike the portrayal of traditional forensics on television, not all of the answers that investigators seek follow the neatly and readily sequence that happens in a

30-minute TV episode with a clear indicator of *"Mr. Plumb in the Conservatory with the Candlestick."*

The fact is, digital evidence is nestled among multiple data layers, to include log files, operating system artifacts, system registry entries, temporary files, network traffic, and both structured and unstructured data in addition to encrypted, obfuscated, and plain text. For example, take modern digital storage devices such as cell phones and hard drives. They can contain a physical and digital life's worth of information about the user, including "*footprints*" of others using the device under their own accounts or sharing an account.

The user might dually use the device for both personal and business activity and all of this, during analysis, must be traced and committed to a process known as *"timelining"*, i.e., recording activity within an overall chronological context with proper interpretation of relevance of time changes upon artifacts[36]. In addition, these devices can contain millions of user "*fingerprints*" across logs, databases, encrypted data, archives, snapshots, deleted fragments, and metadata — and all of this before we even begin talking about artifacts, logs, and file systems that may not track date and time stamp data at a level suitable for digital forensic interpretation and timelining.

---

[36] Some forensic artifacts have their time stamps affected by user actions, while others are affected by system or software actions generated as a result of user or other interactions and sometimes with time drift *"delays."* Still other artifacts can be impacted and updated with something as simple as an antivirus program scanning files en masse, but not changing its contents. And then there's *"timestomping"*, when an actor alters timestamps of files to make them appear as if they were created outside the incident timeframe, often by years; this can lead to important artifacts being more difficult to find or missed entirely. The proper interpretation and testing of artifacts is part of the science and art of Digital Forensics — knowing when the action that caused a time update can be properly associated with the effect of interest and relevance.

FORENSICS ARTIFACTS OVERVIEW

There are countless examples of how Locard's Exchange Principle applies to digital forensic artifacts, so many that if I were to attempt to cover them thoroughly, they would exceed the chapters and scope of this book — perhaps I'll leave that for another book. For the purposes of this moment-in-time writing, I have chosen to focus on a range of Microsoft Windows-based examples because Windows is ultimately one of the most common environments investigated in DFIR.

The following sections attempt, with the best of my intentions, to help readers better understand some of the industry terminology they are likely to encounter in DFIR-related investigations and their resultant reporting. To this end, I have provided high-level technical explanations of what the terms mean and how they relate to answering the important questions of *"what, why, when, where, who, and how"* for executives, counsel, and insurers when a cyber incident strikes.

FILE SYSTEM BASICS

NTFS, or **New Technology File System**, is a system used by Windows computers to organize and manage the files and folders stored on a hard drive or other storage devices. Think of it like a digital filing cabinet [37], where your computer keeps track of where everything is stored, where to locate it within the drawers, and how it's organized. NTFS provides several important features that help keep your data secure and organized, such as **file permissions**, which control who can access or modify files, and built-in **data recovery options**, which can help a user

New Technology File System (NTFS) is a file system developed by Microsoft that has become the standard for Windows-based systems.

It was first introduced with Windows NT 3.1 in 1993 as a replacement for the older FAT (File Allocation Table) file systems. Since the release of Windows XP, NTFS has been the default file system for new installations of Windows.

restore lost or damaged files. Overall, NTFS is an essential part of how a Windows computer stores and manages the data you might rely on every day[38].

The **Master File Table ($MFT)**[39] is a critical component of the NTFS file system, serving as a central index for all files and directories. In our filing cabinet analogy, the $MFT works like the filing cabinet's index or directory.

---

[37] There are some truly great analogies that exist for file systems and many of them center around libraries because those were the analogies that made the most sense in the 90s and early 2000s. I feel, though, that as our generations have progressed, so should our analogies to remain relevant and able to spark the "*Oh yeah! That makes sense*" moment when explaining a complex topic to a jury or a non-technical audience. Which leads me to the analogy of the filing cabinet, also slightly dated by today's standards, but still relatable to most people.
[38] "*Unless you are a crazy person and use a non-Windows product, like an Apple product...*"
[39] Are you wondering why the abbreviation starts with a dollar symbol? Windows files that store metadata (discussed on the next page) all start with the dollar symbol.

This is the list that sits at the top drawer and informs the reader what is inside every folder and where you can find each folder and its contents in the cabinet. Each file and directory on an NTFS volume has a corresponding $MFT entry, known as a **file record**, which contains metadata such as timestamps, file attributes, and pointers to where the file's data is stored. A file record, continuing the prior analogy, is like the label attached to the individual folders in the filing cabinet drawers.

$MFT artifacts can be useful in the following ways:

- **Timestamps:** Each $MFT record contains four (4) timestamps (e.g., creation, modification, $MFT entry modification, and access) that can help investigators establish a timeline of events and identify when malware or other malicious files were created, modified, or accessed.

- **File attributes:** $MFT records store information about a file's attributes, such as hidden or system flags, which can help investigators identify suspicious files that may be attempting to evade detection.

- **Data runs** and **file recovery:** $MFT records contain information about the physical location of file data on disk, known as data runs. This information can help investigators recover deleted or partially overwritten files although it has become increasingly complex over the years as the size of files have grown. For example, if the $MFT records are lost (such as due to ransomware and data encryption), then the ability for a forensic examiner and modern tooling to fully recover intact files of significant data sizes may be near impossible.

- **Resident** and **non-resident data:** In the NTFS file system, the resident portion of a file is the metadata that is stored within the

$MFT, and the non-resident data is the actual file stored on the volume. Examining resident data can help investigators identify relevant file metadata even if the file itself has been deleted or overwritten. I have been part of investigations in the past in which we have identified malware that operated as a sort of fileless malware, where the malicious code was written into the resident portion of the $MFT record itself, hiding among the metadata reserved to describe a legitimate file.

- **The NTFS Journal (USN Journal):** A log of file system changes, such as file creation, deletion, modification, or renaming. It records these events using **Update Sequence Number (USN)** entries, which include information about the type of change, the file's $MFT record index, and the USN entry's timestamp. NTFS Journal artifacts can be useful in three primary ways. First, through **change tracking** — the Journal provides a chronological record of file system changes, which can help investigators identify suspicious activity, such as the creation or modification of malware-related files, or unauthorized access to sensitive data. Second, through **timeline analysis** — correlating Journal entries with other forensic artifacts, such as log files or network traffic data, can help investigators establish a comprehensive timeline of events and uncover connections between seemingly unrelated activities. Third, through **data carving** and **file recovery** — Journal entries can assist in recovering deleted or overwritten files by providing information about the previous state of the file system, which can be combined with $MFT data runs to locate and recover relevant file content.

The wealth of information contained within the $MFT and NTFS Journal can be invaluable to examiners for understanding the scope and nature of an intrusion or malicious activity on a computer system. In addition to the $MFT and NTFS Journal, there are other NTFS file system artifacts and information that are relevant to Digital Forensics and Incident Response and specifically malware-focused aspects of these types of investigations.

Let's walk through some specific examples together.

Alternate Data Streams (ADS) is a feature of NTFS that allows the attachment of metadata to files at a file system level, invisible to normal users, and all without affecting the data content or the file itself. Each file on an NTFS volume is composed of one or more data streams. The data stream that users usually interact with is called the primary data stream and is what you see when you open a file — the presentation of the file's contents itself. It contains the content (text, pictures, executable code, etc.) that the file was created to hold. However, NTFS also allows files to have additional named data streams, where extra data can be associated with a file to describe, support, or define the file itself. These are called alternate data streams. In the eyes of the user and many utilities, the file appears to be unchanged. This can be useful, but can also be exploited for malicious purposes as some antivirus utilities do not scan ADS[40].

For example, create and save a Word Document to your desktop named **redliw.docx** containing the words *"Devon's book 'Diving In — An Incident Responder's Journey' is the best book ever and taught me about the Intrusion Lifecycle and the Engagement Lifecycle plus so much more!"*[41] Now, the Word document you created, with the words you saved within it, are stored in the primary data stream – the file itself. When you close, access, print, or interact with the file,

---

[40] Alternate Data Streams were introduced in NTFS 3.1 and allowed storage of Macintosh Hierarchical File System (HFS) resource forks for files stored between Windows and Mac systems, which stored other file-related data.
[41] Aww, you are too kind.

you are accessing the primary data stream. The filename that you see presented to you via Windows Explorer is actually the name of the primary data stream (the file itself).

Now take that same file and right-click the file, left-click **Properties**, and view the **Summary** information on the file's **Properties** dialog box in Windows (like **Title, Subject, Author,** etc.). What you are viewing is data stored in an ADS, not the file itself (or its primary data stream). Let's continue with this document you created. The File Preview feature in modern versions of Windows is an example of attaching a preview graphic or image, showing the contents of the file, as an ADS to the actual file. The preview image is not part of the primary data stream because you did not create it, the Windows operating system did it for you.

Now let us say that you attach this Word Document to a blog post on your favorite website or a social media posting to, of course, tell all of your friends how great this book is, and you want them to get a copy also for themselves. When they download your shared document file from the internet using a web browser like Microsoft Edge, Google Chrome, or Mozilla Firefox on Windows, an ADS is attached to the file, which contains information about the source of the file, to include identifying that it was downloaded from the internet and can trigger a warning in the case of suspicious files or malware.

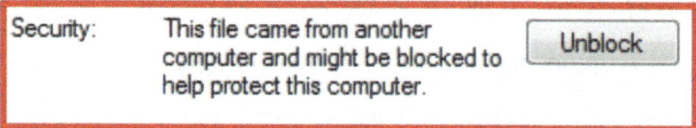

So, let us take your document file through one last hypothetical situation and one that I have observed threat actors leveraging with malware during certain campaigns (although traditionally more with executables, i.e., binaries). You could take and randomly name a document **redliw.docx** and attach hidden content in an ADS randomly named **regiznad**. While there are a few ways to do this, I'll provide the example leveraging PowerShell[42]:

`powershell Set-Content -Path "redliw.docx:regiznad" -Value "This is hidden"`

In this case, **redliw.docx** is the primary data stream and **regiznad** is functioning as an ADS. The text *"This is hidden in an Alternate Data Stream"* is not visible when viewing **redliw.docx** Microsoft Word or via file preview. It can only be accessed by specifically referring to **redliw.docx:regiznad**.

To read the content of an ADS using PowerShell, one could use the command: `powershell Get-Content -Path "redliw.docx:regiznad"`

This command would then display on screen the text you had previously added to the ADS *"This is hidden"*, which is the content of the ADS **regiznad** associated with **redliw.docx**. This is an example of a file system mechanism that was designed for completely normal file enhancement and feature usage, but has been and continues to be misused by actors to obfuscate data or code.

Let us dive deeper into the technical weeds of the most common NTFS aspects that forensic examiners rely upon during Incident Response investigations when building their timelines and conduct their investigative analysis.

- **$SECURE** is a hidden system file in NTFS that contains security descriptors for all files and directories in an NTFS volume. A security descriptor is a data structure that contains the security information associated with a securable object, which can be any object that supports access control, such as files or directories.

---

[42] PowerShell is a native component of the Windows operating system used by administrators. For this reason, a malicious PowerShell script is potentially less likely to be detected than other attacker methods.

- **$LogFile** is a hidden system file in NTFS used for journaling of data and plays a crucial role in the NTFS recovery capabilities. The $LogFile records all transactions that take place within the file system, such as file creation, deletion, movement, renaming, and changes to file attributes. Each of these operations is logged as a transaction in the $LogFile before it's actually performed. If a system crash or power failure occurs during a transaction, the NTFS uses the $LogFile during the system restart to roll back any incomplete transactions and bring the file system back to a consistent state. This resilience process is known as **recovery** and helps prevent data loss and file system corruption that could otherwise occur due to incomplete transactions.

- **$I30 attribute** is an index allocation attribute associated with directories on NTFS volumes, which contains a sorted list of file names and their corresponding $MFT record numbers. Analyzing $I30 attributes can help investigators identify suspicious or malicious files that may be related to an intrusion or malware infection.

- **$MFTMirr** is a partial copy of the $MFT, a type of mirror, used to ensure the integrity of the file system. Comparing the $MFTMirr with the primary MFT can help investigators detect tampering or corruption in the $MFT, which may be indicative of malware or threat actor activity.

- **Volume Shadow Copy Service (VSS)** is a feature in Windows that creates snapshots of NTFS volumes at specific points in time, allowing for the recovery of previous versions of files and directories. Investigating Volume Shadow Copies can help recover earlier versions of files that may have been modified or deleted by malware or threat actors or uncover traces of their activity that have since been overwritten.

- **$Recycle.Bin** folder is used to store deleted files and folders on NTFS volumes until they are permanently removed or restored. Examining the contents of the $Recycle.Bin folder can help investigators recover deleted files or uncover evidence of malicious activity, such as attempts to remove traces of an intrusion or malware infection.

- Windows automatically creates **LNK (shortcut)** files when a user opens a file or accesses a network share. LNK files contain metadata about the target file, such as its file path, creation timestamp, and access timestamp. Analyzing LNK files can help investigators trace user activity, identify suspicious or malicious files that were accessed, and establish a timeline of events.

By examining these artifacts, and many others, Digital Forensics investigators can gain a more comprehensive understanding of the actions performed by malware or threat actors on a computer system. This information can help them establish connections between seemingly unrelated activities, recover critical evidence, and assess the scope and impact of a cyber incident.

WEB BROWSER BASICS

The ubiquitous web browser, probably used nearly as much as your favorite email application or social media app, is a software application that allows you to access and navigate the internet. Its basically a virtual window that lets you view and interact with websites stored on web-servers stored anywhere in the world, helping you find information, watch videos, shop online, or connect with others on social media. Web browsers, such as Chrome, Firefox, Safari, or Edge (which at the time of this writing is basically Chrome under the hood), make it easy to explore the vast world of the internet by converting complex web code into user-friendly pages for point and click interactions with a mouse. Forensically relevant web browser artifacts can provide valuable insights into a user's browsing history, which can be essential when investigating incidents involving watering hole attacks [43], Google ad poisoning attacks [44], phishing email link click-thru events, or social engineering through phishing chat sessions [45]. The following are some key web browser artifacts that can be analyzed during a Digital Forensics' investigation.

---

[43] Explained more in Chapter 6 when discussing the Turla threat actor group and some of their observed tactics.
[44] "Threat Actors use Google Ads to Deploy VIDAR Stealer," Wojcieszek, K., Truman, D., Green, S., & Glass, G. (2022, December 13). Kroll. www.kroll.com/en/insights/publications/cyber/threat-actors-google-ads-deploy-vidar-stealer
[45] "Phishing in New Waters: Exploiting Live Chat to Deliver Malware," Ackerman, D., & Knutson, A. (2021, June 23). Kroll. www.kroll.com/en/insights/publications/cyber/phishing-schemes-online-chat-malware

BROWSING HISTORY

Web browser history is a record of the webpages a user has visited, including the URLs, page titles, and timestamps of when the pages were accessed. Browser history can be of forensic value for several reasons:

- **Evidence of activity:** Web browser history provides valuable insights into a user's online activities and interactions with specific websites or services, which can be crucial when investigating a potential security incident or understanding a user's behavior.

- **Timeline construction:** Browser history typically includes timestamps that help establish a timeline of user activities and correlate events during an investigation.

- **Uncovering hidden or deleted content:** Analyzing web browser history can help uncover content or webpages that have been deleted, removed, or are no longer accessible online, which may be relevant to an investigation.

- **Identifying malicious websites:** Examining browser history can help identify instances where a user may have visited a website hosting malware or other malicious content, which could have compromised the system or contributed to a security incident.

For a real-world example of how analyzing web browser history can deliver important evidence, let's consider the 2015 *United States v. Ross William Ulbricht* case[46], also known as the Silk Road case. The FBI conducted a forensic examination of Ulbricht's laptop, using web browser history as a key piece of evidence during the trial. The browser history revealed that Ulbricht

---

[46] United States v. Ulbricht, No. 14-cr-68 (KBF) (S.D.N.Y. Jan. 7, 2015). https://casetext.com/case/united-states-v-ulbricht-5

had accessed various websites, resources, and chats associated with the administration of the Silk Road, an online marketplace for illegal drugs and other illicit goods. Web browser history analysis uncovered evidence that ultimately assisted in the court case against Ulbricht leading to a successful conviction by the prosecution following a four-week jury trial in February 2015 on seven offenses related to his management of the Silk Road online marketplace. The offenses included distribution of narcotics, distribution of narcotics by means of the internet, conspiring to distribute narcotics, engaging in a continuing criminal enterprise, conspiring to commit computer hacking, conspiring to traffic in false identity documents, and conspiring to commit money laundering. In addition to the life sentence prison term handed down, Ulbricht, aka *"Dread Pirate Roberts"*, was ordered to forfeit $183,961,921[47].

---

[47] "Ross Ulbricht, aka Dread Pirate Roberts, sentenced to life in federal prison for creating, operating 'Silk Road' website". U.S. Immigration and Customs Enforcement (ICE). (2015, May 29). www.ice.gov/news/releases/ross-ulbricht-aka-dread-pirate-roberts-sentenced-life-federal-prison-creating

COOKIES

Cookie files, or simply **cookies** are small text files that web browsers store on a user's computer on behalf of websites. They contain data that websites use to maintain user-specific information, such as login sessions, preferences, or tracking user behavior across different pages or visits. Cookies are interesting in Digital Forensics and Incident Response for several reasons:

1. **User identification:** Cookies often store unique identifiers or tokens[48] that can be used to track a user's browsing habits or associate their activities with a specific account or device. This information can be valuable when profiling a user or investigating a potential security incident.

2. **Login sessions:** Cookies frequently store authentication tokens, which allow users to remain logged in to websites across multiple visits. Analyzing these tokens and their potential misuse against web server login pages, can help investigators determine if an account was compromised or used in unauthorized ways.

3. **Timestamps**: Cookies may include timestamps indicating when they were created or last accessed, which can help establish a timeline of user activities and correlate events during an investigation.

4. **Third-party tracking:** Some cookies are set by third-party services or advertisers for tracking and analytics purposes. Analyzing these cookies can provide insights into a user's interactions with various

---

[48] A "token" is like a digital ID badge. When you log into a website, the website gives your computer this token, which your browser stores as a cookie. This token confirms your identity to the website every time you visit, so you don't have to log in every single time or so that it can remember your site preferences. Think of it as a "remember me" pass that allows the website to recognize you, uniquely from any other user on the internet, and keep you logged in.

websites and services, even if they do not belong to the same domain. Think of this like pollen, mud, or grass that has attached to a person's shoe that can tell a traditional forensic story of where they have walked and been in the past.

CACHE FILES

Cache files are temporary copies of webpages, images, and other content that a web browser stores on a user's computer to improve browsing performance for the next time that the website is visited. Pieces, fragments, portions, or entire webpages are downloaded and *"cached"* on a user's computer and those portions can be, in some cases, re-assembled to form versions of the visited websites from the perspective of the user at the time the computer visited and interacted with a website. This is different from web browser history in that history is only an entry in a database of a website address having been visited and when combined with the available cache, can provide the version of the page viewed or accessed at that time. From a DFIR perspective, web browser cache can be relevant for several reasons:

1. **Evidence of activity:** Cache files can provide insights into a user's browsing history, as they reveal which webpages or content the user has accessed. This information can be instrumental when trying to understand a user's behavior.

2. **Recovering content:** Cache files can help recover content that has been deleted or removed from a website, which could be relevant to an investigation. This includes images, videos, or text that may no longer be available online.

3. **Malware and malicious content:** Examining cache files can help identify instances where a user may have visited a website hosting malware or other malicious content, such as a phishing website, which could have compromised the user's credentials or contributed to a security incident.

4. **Timestamps**: Cache files typically include timestamps, which can help establish a timeline of user activities and correlate events during an investigation.

There have been several court cases over recent years in which a suspect's web browser history played a crucial role, but one in particular of interest was the trial of Scott Peterson in 2004, *The People of the State of California v. Scott Peterson*. Peterson was charged with the murder of his wife, Laci Peterson, and their unborn son in Modesto, California. During the investigation, investigating law enforcement discovered that Peterson had made several internet searches related to currents and fishing in the San Francisco Bay area around the time of Laci's disappearance. Investigators also found evidence of Peterson researching and looking up information on boat ramps in the area. This, combined with other evidence documented in the trial's transcripts, helped investigators place Peterson in the area where his wife's body was later found. It also helped the prosecution to establish premeditation, a key element in a first-degree murder charge.

Consider the 2009 case of *United States v. Kevin Bollaert*[49] where cache files were key in an investigation. Bollaert was the owner and operator of a *"revenge porn"* website, where intimate and private images of individuals were posted without their consent, often accompanied by personal information. Victims could only remove the images by paying a fee to another website, also owned by Bollaert. Law enforcement officials analyzed Bollaert's web browser cache, which contained images from the revenge porn site, as well as login credentials, and fragments of emails from his Gmail account, that directly tied him to the illicit operation. This evidence, along with other pieces of

---

[49] Office of the Attorney General. (2023). Arrest warrant [PDF file]. State of California Department of Justice. https://oag.ca.gov/system/files/attachments/press_releases/Arrest%20warrant_0.pdf

information detailed throughout the trial's transcripts, ultimately led to Bollaert's conviction where he was found guilty on 27 felony counts. It took a court clerk 20 minutes to read the list of convictions against 28-year-old Kevin Bollaert, guilty of 21 identity theft and 6 extortion counts. The web browser cache proved to be a valuable resource in this investigation, providing crucial evidence needed by the prosecutors.

DOWNLOAD HISTORY

Download history is a record of files and content that a user has downloaded through their web browser and can be useful to an investigator in many ways:

1. **Evidence of activity:** Download history can provide valuable insights into a user's online activities and interactions with specific websites or services.

2. **Malware and malicious files:** Examining download history can help identify instances where a user may have inadvertently downloaded malware or other malicious files, which could have compromised the system or contributed to a security incident.

3. **Intellectual property theft:** Download history can be useful in cases involving intellectual property theft or unauthorized access to sensitive information. By examining the files a user has downloaded, an investigator may find evidence of stolen data or other illicit activities.

4. **Policy violations:** In organizational settings, analyzing download history can help identify violations of acceptable use policies or other rules governing the use of company resources.

I had an investigation years ago in which a user's computer was found to be the earliest system of interest in our forensics timeline; it appeared to be where a threat actor's malware and lateral movement in the client's network began. While conducting the forensics review, we were able to locate a key date and time in the user's Chrome browser download history that tied to a specific document of interest. Artifacts cross-correlated with other evidence present on the system to indicate that the file had been opened twice, approximately 37 seconds apart[50]. Following both interactions with the document, a scripting process had been initiated through the simple opening of the document. The script automatically downloaded a file from the internet (more specifically a remote server) in an automated fashion to the computer, hidden from the user's view, that was an initial piece of malware allowing a threat actor command-and-control access to the system (first stage downloader).

The document no longer existed on the system at the time of investigation because the user had deleted and emptied their Recycle Bin to clear the file out. We exhausted forensic avenues for recovering the file, including reviewing restore points, with negative results. Based upon the timeline and findings though, I was able to suggest review of the user's business email account in the client's Microsoft 365 tenant, to include a review of the server-side trash. The original email was identified and successfully recovered, which filled in the missing puzzle pieces for the forensics timeline. The email contained a link that redirected the user to a faux password-protected website. The password was simple and included in the email body. Upon entering the password, the user's web browser automatically received a downloaded file masquerading as an invoice, which contained the script that initiated a download of a malicious file, exactly as the forensics timeline played out on the user's computer.

---

[50] *"Humans Are Notoriously Naïve And Hopeful."* It is common for nontechnical computer users to inadvertently open malicious files, unknowingly, multiple times because they/we want to be trusting human beings and for the non-technical, if they receive an email that provides instructions to open > click a #thing > and be presented with an invoice or redirected to a *"secure login page,"* well, that is what the user is expecting. When it does not present what they were expecting, the percentage of times that I have seen users open the file multiple times, expecting a different outcome, is greater than 50%. Unfortunately, for many malicious files that are script-enabled or embedded, which execute maliciousness in the background without the user's knowledge, the innocent act of repeatedly opening causes **The Kroll Intrusion Lifecycle™** to kick off in earnest (further discussed in Chapter 5).

WEB FORM DATA AND SAVED PASSWORDS

Web form data refers to the information users enter into online forms, such as names, addresses, email addresses, phone numbers, and other personal details. Saved passwords are the login credentials users store within their web browsers to automatically pre-fill and log into websites without re-entering their username and password each time. Both web form data and saved passwords can be of forensic value for several reasons:

1. **Identifying personal information:** Web form data may contain valuable personal information about a user, which can be used to build a profile of the individual and their online activities. This information can be crucial when investigating a potential security incident or understanding a user's behavior.

2. **Accessing user accounts:** Saved passwords can help investigators, given appropriate legal process, access a user's accounts on various websites, which may provide additional evidence or insights into the user's actions or intentions.

3. **Uncovering unauthorized access:** Analyzing saved passwords can help determine if patterns and password re-use is common and assist in determining if an account was compromised or accessed by unauthorized individuals, which could be an indication of a security incident or data breach.

4. **Correlating user activity:** The combination of web form data and saved passwords can help link user activity across different websites

or services, which may be useful when trying to establish a timeline or correlate events during an investigation.

By analyzing the contents of web form data and saved passwords in both Chrome and Firefox, investigators can gather valuable information about a user's online activities, interactions with various websites, and the security of those accounts. In a real-world example, web form data and saved passwords played a significant role during the investigation of the 2010 *United States v. Faisal Shahzad* case[51]. Shahzad was behind the attempted bombing in Times Square, New York City. Upon his arrest, investigators conducted a forensic examination of his laptop and discovered saved passwords, web form data, email login credentials, emails, and chat logs[52]. This allowed investigators access to vital evidence, including communications with his Pakistani Taliban handlers and Faisal's history of searching for information, including videos, on bomb-making materials[53]. This evidence, along with other information, ultimately led to Shahzad's conviction on multiple charges, including attempted use of a weapon of mass destruction and conspiracy to commit an act of terrorism. The web form data and saved passwords provided investigators with a valuable resource, helping to uncover critical evidence and bring Shahzad to justice.

---

[51] "Faisal Shahzad Sentenced in Manhattan Federal Court to Life in Prison for Attempted Car Bombing in Times Square", Federal Bureau of Investigation. (2010, October 5). https://archives.fbi.gov/archives/newyork/press-releases/2010/nyfo100510.htm
[52] U.S. District Court for the Southern District of New York, Transcript of Trial Proceedings, United States v. Faisal Shahzad, 1:10-cr-00942, 2010 WL 4827600 (S.D.N.Y. Nov. 16, 2010)
[53] "Times Square bomber planned second attack, says U.S." Katz, B. Reuters. (2010, September 30). www.reuters.com/article/us-timessquare/times-square-bomber-planned-second-attack-says-u-s-idUSTRE68S50120100930

LOCAL STORAGE AND INDEXEDDB

Local Storage and Indexed Database (IndexedDB) are client-side storage technologies that web applications can use to store data persistently in a user's browser and can be interesting for several reasons:

1. **User data storage:** Web applications may store user-specific data in Local Storage or IndexedDB, such as preferences, authentication tokens, or even personal information. Analyzing this data can help investigators understand user behavior, recover important information, or identify potential data leaks.

2. **Malicious use:** Cybercriminals may exploit these storage technologies to persistently store malicious payloads, exfiltrate data, or maintain control over a compromised system. Investigating these storage areas may help uncover security breaches or indicators of compromise.

3. **Evidence of activity:** The data stored in Local Storage and IndexedDB can provide insights into user activities and interactions with specific websites or services. This information can be valuable when profiling a user or investigating a potential security incident.

By analyzing the contents of Local Storage and IndexedDB[54] in both Chrome and Firefox, a Digital Forensics investigator can gather valuable information about a user's interactions with web applications. For example, the 2020

---

[54] Each subfolder contains IndexedDB databases in LevelDB format. LevelDB format is a simple, lightweight, and efficient way to store and organize data on a computer. It is a type of key-value storage system, which means it stores information in pairs: a unique key (like an identifier or name) and a corresponding value (like a piece of data or information). LevelDB is designed to be fast and scalable, making it well-suited for various applications, including web browsers and other software that need to store large amounts of data quickly and efficiently.

EvilQuest ransomware/spyware combination that was found to be infecting macOS systems through pirated software demonstrated how web browser local storage and IndexedDB could be targeted. EvilQuest, also known as ThiefQuest[55], was a sophisticated piece of malware that contained spyware, keylogging, and ransomware components. Not only could it encrypt files on infected macOS systems, it also exfiltrated sensitive data to the attacker's servers. It could target passwords and web browser related data[56]. Forensic investigators analyzed the malware's behavior and discovered that it was specifically designed to access and exfiltrate passwords as well as cryptocurrency wallet data (if present on the system), and run in the background, keylogging and listening for credit card numbers and other financial information to be typed into web forms on e-commerce websites.

Web applications that can store data persistently in a user's web browser are online tools or services that save specific information directly in your browser so that it remains available even after you close the browser or restart your computer. This allows the web application to remember your preferences, settings, or any other data that it needs to function effectively, and to quickly access that data the next time you visit the website. Examples include online shopping carts that remember items you have added, personalized website layouts, or online games that save your progress. These applications help improve your online experience by providing a more tailored and efficient interaction with the websites you use regularly. However, this ability to store data persistently can also be exploited by malware or malicious processes. Cybercriminals may use maliciously crafted web applications to store harmful

---

[55] ""EvilQuest" Rolls Ransomware, Spyware & Data Theft Into One", Phil Stokes, SentinelOne. July 8, 2020. www.sentinelone.com/blog/evilquest-a-new-macos-malware-rolls-ransomware-spyware-and-data-theft-into-one
[56] Goodin, D. July 1, 2020. New Mac ransomware is even more sinister than it appears. Ars Technica. https://arstechnica.com/information-technology/2020/07/new-mac-ransomware-is-even-more-sinister-than-it-appears

code or payloads for loading and delivery through your browser, which can then execute without your knowledge, compromising your device or stealing sensitive information. A real-world example of a web application being used maliciously is the Magecart[57] attacks. Magecart are a group of cybercriminals that target online shopping websites by injecting malicious code into the web application. This code, often called a "*skimmer*," steals customers' credit card information when they enter it on the compromised website. The skimmer can persistently store this stolen data in the user's browser and transmit it to the attackers' server, allowing for the collection of sensitive information from numerous victims without being detected. Another historical and rather hilarious example was the Samy worm, a cross-site scripting (XSS) worm that was created in 2005 by a user named Samy Kamkar. He exploited a vulnerability in the MySpace social networking platform to inject malicious JavaScript code into his profile. When other users visited his profile, the code executed in their browsers and added Samy as their friend, while also copying the malicious code to their profiles. The worm spread quickly, infecting over a million MySpace[58] users within a few hours.

---

[57] www.kroll.com/en/insights/publications/cyber/monitor/what-is-magecart-malware-how-to-protect-against-it
[58] "*Okay Boomer...MySpace...You must be old...*"

EXTENSION DATA

Web browser extensions in both Google Chrome and Mozilla Firefox can be interesting:

1. **Data access:** Extensions can have wide-ranging permissions to access and modify the user's browsing data, such as browsing history, cookies, bookmarks, and even passwords. This can be valuable for investigators to understand user behavior, track malicious extensions, or recover important information.

2. **Malicious extensions:** Some extensions may be intentionally malicious, designed to steal user data, serve as adware, or execute other harmful actions. Identifying these extensions can help uncover security breaches, potential data leaks, or unauthorized access to sensitive information.

3. **User behavior and interests:** Extensions can provide insights into a user's interests and online habits, as they are typically installed to enhance or customize the browsing experience. This information may be relevant to an investigation, especially if it involves profiling the user or understanding their online behavior.

4. **Evidence of activity:** Since extensions may interact with specific websites or services, they can potentially serve as evidence of user activity related to those sites or services. For example, an extension for a specific social media platform may indicate frequent use of that platform.

By examining the contents of the **Extensions** folder in Chrome and the **extensions** folder in Firefox, as well as analyzing extension files and manifest files (**manifest.json** for Chrome and **install.rdf** or **manifest.json** for

Firefox), a Digital Forensics investigator can gather valuable information about the user's installed extensions and their potential impact on the user's browsing activities. This information can aid in Incident Response efforts and contribute to a better understanding of the scope and nature of a security incident.

BROWSER CONFIGURATION FILES

These configuration files store browser settings and preferences. Examining them can help identify any unauthorized changes made by an attacker, such as modifying proxy settings or disabling security features. These files contain valuable information that can help move an investigation forward:

- **Network traffic analysis:** In conjunction with browser artifacts, investigators can analyze network traffic data (e.g., captured via Wireshark or extracted from firewall logs) to identify connections to malicious websites or servers, which may be indicative of a watering hole attack, Google ad poisoning attack, or phishing email link.

- **DNS cache analysis:** By examining the system's DNS cache, investigators can identify any malicious domain names that the user's computer resolved (i.e., connected to), which may be related to a network intrusion.

By leveraging these additional artifacts and techniques, Digital Forensics investigators can further enhance their understanding of the user's activities and the nature of the attack. The information gleaned from these artifacts can help identify key evidence, such as malicious URLs, files, or domain names, and uncover insights into the attacker's tactics, techniques, and procedures (TTPs). Ultimately, this knowledge can aid in the development of more effective Incident Response strategies and contribute to the overall security posture of an organization.

REGISTRY BASICS

The Windows Registry is a hierarchical database that stores configuration settings and options for the Windows operating system, applications, hardware, and user preferences. It contains a wealth of information that can be valuable for Digital Forensics investigations. The Registry is organized into several main sections called **hives**, which store data in separate files. Think of the Registry as a massive filing cabinet, and the registry hives are the individual drawers within the cabinet.[59] From a Digital Forensics' perspective, the following Registry hives are considered forensically relevant and meaningful:

- **HKEY_LOCAL_MACHINE (HKLM):** This hive contains information about the computer's hardware and system settings, including device drivers, services, and startup programs. The associated files for this hive include **SYSTEM, SOFTWARE, SAM, SECURITY, COMPONENTS,** and **DRIVERS**.
- **HKEY_USERS (HKU):** This hive stores user-specific settings, such as desktop backgrounds, software, and application preferences. Each user profile on the system has its own registry hive, stored as a individual **NTUSER.DAT** files within each user profile directory.

These Registry hives can be useful to identify and locate evidence of a threat actor or malware on a computer during an investigation in several ways:

- **User activity:** HKU hives store user-specific settings and preferences, which can provide insights into user activity on the

---

[59] Microsoft likes to compare the Registry to a tree, with nodes, aka "keys" that branch off. You can learn more about how the Registry is structured here: https://learn.microsoft.com/en-us/windows/win32/sysinfo/structure-of-the-registry

system. For example, investigators can analyze the **UserAssist** key[60] to determine which applications a user has executed and when.

- **Malware persistence:** Many malware variants establish persistence on a system by creating or modifying Registry keys. For example, malware may create an entry in the **\Run**[61] key to ensure it is executed at system startup. Identifying these keys that are read from during system start can help investigators uncover malware infections and understand persistence mechanisms.

- **System configuration and changes:** The **HKLM** hive contains data about system settings, installed software, and hardware configuration. Analyzing this data can help investigators identify unauthorized changes to the system or the presence of malicious software.

- **Logon and authentication data:** The **HKLM\SAM** and **HKLM\SECURITY** hives store information about user accounts and security settings, including password hashes and group membership data. Investigators can use this information to identify potentially compromised accounts or unauthorized access attempts.

- **Network activity:** Registry keys such as **HKLM\SYSTEM\CurrentControlSet\Services\Tcpip\Parameters** store information about the system's network configuration and activity. Analyzing this data can help investigators identify unauthorized connections, changes to network settings, or evidence of command-and-control (C2) communication.

- **File and program associations:** Registry keys in both the **HKLM** and **HKU** hives store data about file type associations and registered

---

[60] HKU<UserSID>\Software\Microsoft\Windows\CurrentVersion\Explorer\UserAssist
[61] HKLM\SOFTWARE\Microsoft\Windows\CurrentVersion\Run

applications. For example, the **HKLM\SOFTWARE\Classes** key contains information about file extensions and their associated programs. Identifying unusual or malicious file associations can help investigators uncover evidence of malware or threat actor activity.

- **Timestamps:** Many Registry keys contain LastWrite timestamps, which indicate when the key was last modified. These timestamps can help investigators establish a timeline of events and correlate Registry data with other system artifacts.

By examining the forensically relevant Registry hives, Digital Forensics investigators can gain insights into user and system activities, uncover evidence of malware or threat actor activity, and establish a more complete understanding of events that occurred during an incident.

WINDOWS EVENT LOG BASICS

Windows Event Logs are an integral part of the Microsoft Windows operating system, designed to record a wide range of system, security, and application-related events. A Windows Event Log is like a detailed diary or journal for your computer. It keeps a meticulous record of all significant events and activities happening within the system, such as software installations and updates, hardware changes, and security events, noting the time they occurred and providing a brief description.

These Event Logs provide a centralized logging mechanism that helps system administrators and Digital Forensics investigators monitor and analyze system behavior, diagnose issues, and identify potential security incidents. These records can be especially helpful when troubleshooting issues or investigating potential security concerns, as they offer valuable insights into what happened, when it happened, and how it may have affected your computer.

From a Digital Forensics' perspective, Windows Event Logs can be useful to identify and locate evidence of a threat actor or malware on a computer during an investigation in several ways:

- **Event log categories:** Windows Event Logs are divided into multiple categories, such as System, Security, and Application logging. Each category records specific types of events that can provide valuable information for a forensic investigation. For example, Security logs contain events related to user authentication and access control, while Application logs record events generated by installed applications.

- **Event IDs:** Each event logged in the Windows Event Logs has a unique Event ID associated with it. Event IDs help investigators to identify and filter specific events of interest. For example, Event ID 4624 corresponds to a successful Windows User Account logon, while Event ID 4688 indicates the creation of a new process[62].
- **Timestamps:** Windows Event Logs store timestamp information for each recorded event, which can help investigators establish a timeline of activities and correlate events with other forensic artifacts. Timestamps can be crucial in understanding the sequence of actions taken by a threat actor or malware on the system.
- **User and system information:** Windows Event Logs contain information about the user account and system context associated with a particular event. This data can help investigators identify which user accounts were involved in specific activities and determine the scope of a threat actor's access or malware infection. Windows Event Logs often include detailed information about the event, such as process names, file paths, Registry keys, IP addresses, and more. This data can help investigators pinpoint specific actions taken during an intrusion by a threat actor or deployed malware, identify indicators of compromise (IOCs), and uncover chronological pieces that allow investigators to tell the story of what happened.

---

[62] In the context of a Windows operating system, a process is essentially a program that is currently running on a computer. For example, when you open an application, such as Microsoft Word or your web browser, the operating system creates a process for that application. Each process has its own dedicated portion of the system's memory and runs independently of other processes. A process can also spawn multiple "*sub-processes*" or "*threads*" to perform different tasks simultaneously. For example, in a web browser, each tab you open might be a separate thread within the browser's process. In simple terms, you can think of a process as a worker who is carrying out a task (running a program) on your computer.

- **Log retention and persistence**: Windows Event Logs persist across system reboots and can be configured to retain data for extended periods. This persistence enables investigators to analyze historical event data, which can be vital in uncovering evidence of past intrusions or malicious activity.
- **Log collection and analysis tools**: Various tools can be used to collect, filter, and analyze Windows Event Logs, such as Event Viewer, PowerShell[63] cmdlets (e.g., Get-WinEvent), or third-party log analysis tools. These tools can help investigators efficiently sift through large volumes of event data and identify events of interest.

By examining Windows Event Logs, Digital Forensics investigators can gain insights into user and system activities, establish a timeline of events, and uncover crucial evidence related to the actions of a threat actor or malware during a cyber incident. The wealth of information contained within these logs can be invaluable in understanding the scope and nature of an intrusion or malicious activity on a computer system.

---

[63] We briefly introduced PowerShell back in Chapter 3 and noted that a PowerShell script is potentially less likely to be detected than other attacker methods. Here's why: PowerShell is a command-line shell and scripting language developed by Microsoft for task automation and configuration management on Windows and other operating systems. It provides a command-line interface (CLI) for interacting with various system components and applications, as well as a scripting language that allows users to automate tasks and create custom functions and modules. PowerShell uses a combination of command-line syntax and .NET programming concepts, including object-oriented programming, to provide a powerful and flexible environment for system administration, automation, and management. It also supports remote administration, allowing administrators to manage systems and devices from a centralized location. PowerShell is designed to be an extensible platform, with support for custom modules and third-party extensions.

EVENT TRACING FOR WINDOWS BASICS

Event Tracing for Windows (ETW) is a high-performance, low-overhead logging mechanism built into the Microsoft Windows operating system. It provides a unified infrastructure for capturing and storing kernel-level and application-level events, performance data, and diagnostic information.

ETW is like a sophisticated security camera system. It constantly monitors various components and activities on a Windows system, capturing detailed information about performance, errors, and other events in real-time. Imagine your computer as a bustling shopping mall, with different stores representing various software applications and services. The ETW system acts as a network of cameras placed throughout the mall, observing and recording everything that happens, from customer foot traffic and sales transactions to maintenance work and security incidents. Just as a mall manager would rely on security camera footage to investigate an incident or improve customer experience, IT professionals can review the "*footage*" collected by ETW to monitor system and application behavior, gain insights into how different components interact, identify bottlenecks, and detect issues that may have gone unnoticed.

From a Digital Forensics' perspective, ETW can be useful in finding evidence of threat actors on a computer system during an investigation in the following ways:

- **Broad coverage of events:** ETW can capture a wide range of events, including system events, application events, and user events. This broad coverage provides investigators with a wealth of information about system and application activity, which can help identify evidence of threat actors.

- **Real-time and historical data:** ETW can be used to capture real-time event data or analyze historical data stored in trace log files (ETL files). This flexibility allows investigators to examine events that occurred during a specific time frame or monitor ongoing activity on a system.

- **Granular data collection:** ETW allows for granular control over which events are collected and stored, enabling investigators to focus on specific event categories, providers [64], or channels that may be relevant to a particular investigation.

- **Correlation with other forensic artifacts:** ETW events often contain data that can be correlated with other forensic artifacts, such as Registry entries, log files, or file system activity. This correlation can help investigators uncover connections between different pieces of evidence and provide a more comprehensive understanding of a threat actor's actions.

An ETW provider is like a reporter that provides specific types of news or information. In the context of a computer system, an ETW provider is a particular source of event data. This could be a software application, a Windows service, a Windows driver, or the operating system itself. These providers generate events - think of these as news stories - about what they're doing. For example, a provider might generate an event when a file is opened, when a network connection is made, or when an error occurs.

---

[64] Microsoft. System ETW Provider Event Keyword/Level Settings. Microsoft Learn. https://learn.microsoft.com/en-us/message-analyzer/system-etw-provider-event-keyword-level-settings

- **Custom event providers**: In addition to built-in event providers, developers can create custom event providers to log application-specific events. This can be useful in investigations involving custom or targeted malware, as it may provide insights into the behavior and capabilities of the threat.

- **Integration with other tools**: ETW data can be consumed and analyzed using various tools, including Windows Performance Analyzer, Windows Performance Recorder, and third-party tools like PerfView or Microsoft Message Analyzer. These tools can help investigators visualize and analyze the collected event data more effectively.

By leveraging ETW in a Digital Forensics investigation, investigators can gain valuable insights into system and application activity, both in real-time and historically. This information can help identify suspicious behavior, uncover evidence related to threat actors, and establish a more complete understanding of the events that occurred during a cyber incident.

PREFETCH BASICS

Prefetch is a feature in Windows that acts like a personal assistant, anticipating your needs and preparing things in advance to help your computer run more efficiently. Imagine your computer as a busy kitchen in a restaurant, where different dishes (software applications) are being prepared by the chef (your computer's processor). The Prefetch feature is like a sous chef who pays attention to the dishes that are frequently ordered and preps the ingredients ahead of time so the chef can quickly assemble and serve those dishes when they're requested. By keeping track of which applications you use most often, Prefetch helps a Windows-based computer "*pre-load*" parts of those programs into memory before you even open them. This way, when you do need to use the application, it launches faster and feels more responsive, as the system has already done some of the *"recipe prep work"*.

From a Digital Forensics' perspective, prefetch files can be valuable sources of information about the applications that have been executed on a system. They can provide insights into the actions of a threat actor during an investigation. Some of the technical details that make prefetch files useful in a forensic investigation are:

- **File location:** Prefetch files are typically located within a predefined System folder identified as **\Prefetch**.[65]
- **File naming convention:** Prefetch files have a specific naming convention, **[executable name]-[hash].pf**, where the executable name is the name of the application and the hash is a unique identifier generated by the operating system.

---

[65] C:\Windows\Prefetch by default

- **File content:** A prefetch file contains information about the executable file, its associated resources, and the sequence of disk sectors that were accessed during the application launch. This information includes the file path, the number of times the application was executed, and timestamps.
- **Timestamps:** Prefetch files store the timestamps of the last eight (8) times the corresponding application was executed. These timestamps can help investigators establish a timeline of events and determine when a specific application was launched by a threat actor.
- **Frequency of use:** By examining the execution count stored in the prefetch file, investigators can determine how frequently an application was used. This information can help identify suspicious or unusual activity, such as the frequent execution of a rarely used application or the use of tools commonly associated with threat actors.
- **Linking to other artifacts:** The file paths and associated resources stored in prefetch files can help investigators link the execution of an application to other forensic artifacts on the system, such as Registry entries, log files, or recently accessed files. This can help establish connections between different pieces of evidence and provide a more comprehensive understanding of a threat actor's actions.

By analyzing prefetch files, Digital Forensics investigators can gain valuable insights into the applications that were executed on a system, their frequency of use, and the associated timestamps. This information can help investigators identify suspicious activity, establish a timeline of events, and uncover crucial evidence related to the actions of a threat actor during an incident.

SHELLBAG BASICS

Imagine you are walking along a beach, leaving footprints in the sand as you go. These footprints represent a record of your journey: where you have been, how long you have spent in each place, and even which direction you were heading. In an analogous way, Windows Registry Shellbags are like digital footprints left behind by computer users. Whenever you open, access, or modify folders (directories) in your Windows operating system, it leaves a digital trace in the form of Shellbags. These Shellbags contain information about the user's actions, such as which folders they have visited. Just like how footprints in the sand can be analyzed to understand a person's path along a beach, Shellbags can be used to gain insights into a user's directory browsing on local or remote network shares.

This can be particularly helpful for forensic investigators and incident responders who need to understand a user's behavior and directory traversal. Shellbags are stored in the Windows Registry and can provide valuable information for Digital Forensics investigators during an investigation.

- **File and folder access:** By examining Shellbags, investigators can gain insights into the files and folders that the user accessed or interacted with, even if the files or folders have been deleted or moved. This information can help in identifying any suspicious activity or potential evidence related to the threat actor.
- **Timestamps:** Shellbags often contain timestamp information, which can help investigators establish a timeline of user activity. This can be particularly valuable when correlating events or understanding the sequence of actions taken by a threat actor on the system.
- **Persistence:** Since Shellbags are stored in the Windows Registry and persist across reboots and user logins (and are tracked per user account), they provide a reliable source of information for investigators, even if other traces of activity have been removed or modified by the threat actor.
- **Attribution:** In some cases, Shellbags can provide insights into the actions of specific users, as they are stored within each user's Registry hive (**NTUSER.DAT**), of which one should exist per user account on a system, to include networked accounts that have logged on. This can help investigators determine which user account was used by an unauthorized user or threat actor to perform certain actions.

I recall a law enforcement investigation from years ago in which I was on scene as part of a search team executing a search warrant at a subject's location. While Agents from my team were interviewing[66] the subject of our investigation in one room of the residence, I was in the next room over,

---

[66] It is worth noting that the subject was not under arrest at this time, was voluntarily cooperating with law enforcement, and had consented to be interviewed.

working on forensically previewing digital evidence that our search team had been locating and inventorying within the residence.

As I was overhearing bits and pieces of the interview progress, I was previewing the hard drive of a particular laptop and realized that a specific thumb drive had a history of being repeatedly connected to the device historically. Forensic evidence on the device, to include my triage of the primary user account's Shellbags information, indicated files and folders of interest on the thumb drive that matched file names of information of interest to our investigation. Now, my attention became laser-focused on finding this thumb drive.

I had started scratching out notes on my notepad and I had identified an approximately timeline of a Windows user account for my subject logging into the laptop, navigating to a particular website key to our investigation, entering a username and password on the websites, successfully authenticating, and then spending approximately 42 minutes on the website interacting with it. In analyzing that 42-minute-long web browser session, I identified activity on the laptop consistent with files being created (as a result of being downloaded) directly to the thumb drive that I did not yet have access to. In addition, my forensic preview of the available Shellbags information indicated that the user of the computer during this session had navigated to the thumb drive and had opened folders on the thumb drive, as if to check if the files were downloading correctly. In addition, I had prefetch entries during the 42-minute window indicative of two applications, one for opening PDFs and the other for unzipping .ZIP compressed archive files, consistent with file types that had been downloaded from the website.

As I continued my forensic preview of the laptop, I found numerous applications consistent with penetration testing and vulnerability discovery.

One of the Shellbag folder paths that I found interesting recorded navigation by the user to a folder path that indicated a number of folders sorted by web domain names (www.domain.com addresses), such as coastalandsouthernstate.info, hwregiznad_sequences.com, or 2conferencesin2weeks.org[67] etc. Multiple domains in the real list that I identified were companies that had been victims to a specific website vulnerability discovered months earlier. If exploited, these vulnerabilities allowed for unauthorized access and data exfiltration which, through numerous search warrants and subpoenas for information, had led our FBI team to the residence of our subject who was suspected as being responsible for the unauthorized access and data thefts.

Under United States federal statutes, the following are a couple of the most common that federal investigators and prosecutors may operate with:

Computer Fraud and Abuse Act (CFAA) - 18 U.S.C. § 1030: *This is the primary federal law against hacking and unauthorized access. It criminalizes unauthorized access to computers and networks, and it also covers the transmission of harmful code and denial of service attacks.*

Electronic Communications Privacy Act (ECPA) - 18 U.S.C. § 2510-22: *This law protects wire, oral, and electronic communications while those communications are being made, are in transit, and when they are stored on computers. The Act applies to email, telephone conversations, and data stored electronically.*

At this point, I had my timeline sketched out fairly well on my notepad, and I sent a text message to the lead investigator that I had evidence of interest to help with their interview. A few minutes later, the Case Agent walked in,

---

[67] Completely made up by author for example purposes and bear no significance to any legitimate domains that may exist in the future at these addresses.

and I showed him my timeline. I still remember the look on his face as eyes grew wide and a smile appeared on his face realizing that not only did we have the right individual, but what we had found forensically, to include from Shellbags, was exactly what we had been looking for, complete with a timeline of the activity that matched the other sides of our investigation, which had included analysis of the website compromises from the victim perspective as experienced by the victim organizations.

The Case Agent smiled and walked out to resume the interview. As I listened, the subject's stories began to

Under United States federal statutes, the following are a couple of the most common that federal investigators and prosecutors may operate with:

***Wire Fraud Act - 18 U.S.C. § 1343**: This law criminalizes the use of interstate wire communications to defraud someone of property. This can include internet communications and is often used in conjunction with other cybercrime laws.*

***Identity Theft and Assumption Deterrence Act - 18 U.S.C. § 1028**: This law makes it a federal crime when someone "knowingly transfers or uses, without lawful authority, a means of identification of another person with the intent to commit, or to aid or abet, any unlawful activity that constitutes a violation of Federal law, or that constitutes a felony under any applicable State or local law."*

unravel as the Case Agent was able to specifically navigate irrefutable forensic evidence that had been pulled from the subject's own laptop. After about another thirty or so minutes, I remember the moment when the Case Agent walked back into where I was working, walked over to a closet, opened the door, and reached up above the door frame on the inside and lowered his hand with a thumb drive in hand and smiled. Photographs, and appropriate chain-of-custody information and documentation, was completed and upon previewing the thumb drive, I was able to find all of the files and folders that lined up with the Shellbag-derived information from the laptop.

Without the Shellbag and forensic preview of information, that entire interview would have proceeded much differently and it is even possible that the critical piece of evidence that helped catapult our investigation forward might have never been found during our search.

CHAPTER 4 - CAUSALITY & ETHICS

THE RELATIONSHIP BETWEEN CAUSE AND EFFECT

User causality in the context of Digital Forensics science refers to the relationship between a user's actions (**cause**) and the resulting impact on a digital system (**effect**) which fundamentally underpins Locard's Exchange Principle. Understanding this cause-and-effect relationship is a key baseline from which Digital Forensic and Incident Response investigators should operate from.

When threat actors attempt to compromise a system, they perform a series of actions designed to further their access, exploit vulnerabilities, or exfiltrate data. Any of these actions has a specific effect on the targeted system through which they operate, such as obtaining elevated privileges, simply logging into systems with authorized credentials, installing software or executing malware, and even leveraging tooling to steal information and leave the network with it. In this context, user causality defines what threat actors leave behind as their digital fingerprints (or footprints) during every intrusion and what incident responders like myself systematically analyze to identify and document the timeline of the crime.

Digital Forensic investigators rely upon their training, experience, and understanding of digital cause-and-effect relationships to scientifically and defensibly reconstruct chain of events that led to a security incident. By examining the digital artifacts left behind by a threat actor's actions, we investigate the techniques and steps employed, uncovering insights and evidence in a chronological retelling of events.

Several times throughout my career while providing expert testimony during court cases, I and others within the DFIR profession have been asked by defense counsel if we can explain to the jury with definitiveness that the defendant was at the keyboard and conducted the actions that the prosecution claims they did. As professionals, our focus is to answer these types of questions in an educational way focused on the jury's understanding that due to a thorough analysis and review of the preponderance and totality of available evidence, we as investigators were able to establish timelines, interpret forensic artifacts, and combine with user causality actions allowing for the narrowing and focus to the defendant.

The scientific analysis of user causality in Digital Forensics involves the systematic examination of data, the application of training and experience, and the use of deductive and inductive reasoning to establish connections between actions and their consequences, or in other words, actions and their digital reactions within an electronic ecosystem of a computer and its operating system. By adhering to the principles of the scientific method on which Digital Forensics is based, experts can help ensure investigations are thorough, findings are accurate, and potential attributions are reliable, all while remaining independent and dispassionate — the facts are what the facts are.

ETHICAL HANDLING OF ORIGINAL EVIDENCE

The handling of original evidence is a pivotal aspect of Digital Forensics and Incident Response (DFIR), with significant legal and ethical dimensions. While not everything that DFIR practitioners acquire or examine results in evidence that may ever head to court, the fundamental processes of Digital Forensics science should be adhered to in every investigation.

The American Bar Association's Model Rules of Professional Conduct (Rule 3.4)[68] stipulate that attorneys must not unlawfully obstruct another party's access to evidence or unlawfully alter, destroy, or conceal a document or other material having potential evidentiary value. This rule, while formulated for the physical world, holds equal weight in the digital realm, necessitating meticulous handling of original digital evidence to prevent any form of alteration, destruction, or loss. Further, the National Institute of Standards and Technology's (NIST) guidelines for digital evidence preservation[69] underscore the importance of maintaining an unbroken chain of custody and documenting all interactions with the evidence.

Imagine the situation an attorney might find themselves in if a forensics professional did not adhere to proper evidence handling principles. Imagine the attorney's finding out years later that an investigation contained the evidence pivotal in a class action lawsuit, a trademark infringement court case, or a federal trial of a threat actor who caused millions in damages across dozens of victims. From a legal analysis perspective, mishandling original evidence can lead to severe consequences, including the potential exclusion of evidence in court proceedings, admonishment of the attorney and

---

[68] www.americanbar.org/groups/professional_responsibility/publications/model_rules_of_professional_conduct/rule_3_4_fairness_to_opposing_party_counsel
[69] https://nvlpubs.nist.gov/nistpubs/ir/2022/NIST.IR.8387.pdf

investigative teams involved, and worse case even, a mistrial. This could significantly impact the outcome of years' worth of investigation, leading to potential miscarriages of justice and victims being left without restitution or compensation.

Mishandling of evidence can undermine a court's trust in digital forensic science, let alone the testifying professional's training and knowledge of court-acceptable evidence-handling procedures. Practitioners must adhere to established protocols such as creating forensically sound copies of digital evidence, maintaining separate original and derivative evidence copies, using write-blocking processes or tools to prevent changes to original evidence, leveraging cryptographic hashing for verification that evidence remains unchanged and has not been altered during an investigative process, and maintaining proper chain of custody for anyone that interacts with the evidence.

> *Restitution is a legal concept where the offender is required to give up the gains from their wrongdoing to the victim. This can include returning stolen property, paying for damages caused, or compensating for losses incurred as a result of the crime. Compensation, on the other hand, is typically awarded in civil cases and is designed to restore the victim, as much as possible, to the position they were in before the harm occurred. In the context of investigations involving cybercrime, this can include compensation for emotional distress, loss of earnings stemming from business interruption losses, and other forms of financial harm. Both restitution and compensation are forms of "remedies" in the United States' legal system, which are measures designed to enforce a right, impose a penalty, or make another court order. The goal of these remedies is to rectify the harm caused by unlawful or harmful actions, and in doing so, make the victim(s) "whole" again.*

UNDERSTANDING AND INTERPRETING FORENSIC ARTIFACTS

The interpretation of forensic artifacts is a complex task that requires a deep understanding of the causality of artifacts and the tools being used, and proper training and experience to guide in proper interpretation. Practitioners must avoid conjecture and base their interpretations on sound forensic principles and repeatable methodologies. This involves understanding the context in which the digital artifact was created or modified, the actions that impacted that artifact's state, and the implications of its existence. Misinterpretation of forensic causality can lead to false-positive results or negatives, potentially resulting in flawed opinions or conclusions, and even impact follow-on analysis if built upon incorrect data. Ethically, it is incumbent upon practitioners to continually update their knowledge and skillsets so as to ensure accurate interpretation of forensic artifacts.

NEUTRALITY AND FACT-BASED ANALYSIS

DFIR practitioners must remain dispassionate and neutral in their analysis and interpretation of digital evidence. The American Academy of Forensic Sciences' Code of Ethics (Article II, Section 1)[70] emphasizes the importance of impartiality and objectivity in forensic analysis. This means that practitioners must not allow personal beliefs, biases, or preconceived notions to influence their analyses. Bias or preconceived notions can skew analysis and interpretation, leading to flawed conclusions and potentially impacting the outcome of legal proceedings. Ethically, it is imperative for practitioners to approach each investigation with a focus on the facts presented by the evidence. This requires a commitment to rigorous analytical methodologies, a willingness to question assumptions, and a dedication to transparency and documented repeatability of processes throughout the analysis.

---

[70] www.aafs.org/sites/default/files/media/documents/AAFS%20Bylaws-April2021.pdf

In the realm of DFIR, neutrality and fact-based analysis are not just ethical imperatives, but also legal necessities. Courts rely on the impartiality of forensic experts to ensure fair proceedings. Any deviation from neutrality can lead to a miscarriage of justice, undermining the very foundation of the legal system. DFIR practitioners must maintain an unwavering commitment to impartiality, ensuring their analyses are grounded in facts and not influenced by external pressures, client requests, victim pressures, or personal biases. Practitioners must remember that their role is not to prove guilt, but to present an unbiased analysis of the digital evidence. This requires a rigorous, methodical approach, ensuring that every conclusion is supported by concrete evidence and sound reasoning.

In a court case, the role of proving guilt lies with the prosecutor, not the expert witness or the jury. This principle is rooted in the legal concept of "burden of proof," which in criminal cases is always on the prosecution. The prosecutor must present sufficient evidence to convince the jury "beyond a reasonable doubt" that the defendant committed the crime. The role of an expert witness, on the other hand, is to provide independent, objective expertise and opinion to assist the court in understanding technical or complex issues pertinent to the case. The expert's duty is to the court, not to the party who retained them. They must provide unbiased, clear, and comprehensive information within their area of expertise. They do not advocate for either side and are not responsible for proving guilt or innocence. The jury's role is to impartially evaluate the evidence presented by both sides during the trial. They listen to the testimonies, review the evidence, and hear the arguments of the prosecution and the defense. Based on this information, they determine whether the prosecution has met the burden of proof and decide whether the defendant is guilty or not guilty.

USER CAUSALITY DETERMINED FROM DIGITAL EVIDENCE

Understanding user causality — how a user's actions lead to the creation of specific digital artifacts — is a critical aspect of DFIR. Determining user causality often involves delving into private, personal data. DFIR practitioners must balance the need for thorough investigation with respect for privacy rights, a balance that is often legally mandated. For instance, the Fourth Amendment to the U.S. Constitution protects individuals from unreasonable searches and seizures, a principle that extends to digital investigations. From an ethical perspective, DFIR practitioners must ensure that their investigations are proportionate and necessary. Intruding on personal privacy for trivial reasons or without sufficient cause can be seen as unethical. Moreover, practitioners must be careful not to jump to conclusions based on incomplete or out-of-context data. They must remember that correlation does not imply causation — a basic principle of logic that holds true in Digital Forensics.

CHAPTER 5 - THE KROLL INTRUSION LIFECYCLE™

During the early days of computing, viruses were a relatively rare occurrence. The first documented computer virus, called the "*Creeper Virus*,"[71] was written by Bob Thomas at BBN Technologies in 1971 as an experiment in self-replication. It was specifically designed to move between computers on ARPANET, the precursor to the modern-day internet. Creeper worked by copying itself onto the victim's computer and then displaying the message "*I'm the creeper, catch me if you can!*". The virus would then try to find another computer to infect. Creeper was not malicious in nature, and it did not cause any damage to the victim's computer. However, it did cause some disruption, as it would repeatedly display its message and try to infect other computers. In 1971, Ray Tomlinson, who also worked with Bob at BBN Technologies and maintained a friendly rivalry, created Reaper, a program that was designed to hunt down and delete Creeper. Reaper worked by searching for the Creeper virus and then deleting it.

Over the next few decades, to include the early parts of my education and career, viruses continued to be a relatively minor threat. They were typically spread through physical media, such as infected floppy disks, and were relatively easy to detect and remove. However, as the internet's reach and connectivity spread globally, the ever-present poison of human evil and

---

[71] "What is the Creeper Virus?" Techslang. www.techslang.com/definition/what-is-the-creeper-virus

predatory practices followed. One of the key turning points in malware evolution occurred in the early 2000s with the emergence of worms such as Code Red and Nimda[72]. These worms were capable of self spreading rapidly across the internet, infecting thousands of computers in a matter of hours. This marked a shift from viruses that spread through physical media to malware that could spread through network connections.

In addition to their ability to spread quickly, modern malware is also characterized by its command-and-control (C2)[73] capabilities, which has given rise to more complex cyber threats. Threat actors began shifting tactics towards active hands-on command issuance, arguably from anywhere in the world, making it more difficult for law enforcement to track and prosecute. At the same time, this next generation of malware variants has been designed to evade detection by the antivirus and anti-malware software solutions that organizations adopted in the early 2000s to combat the virus threat.

This has led in recent years to the evolution and adoption of endpoint detection and response (EDR)[74] technologies, which build upon the purpose

---

[72] "Net-Worm:W32/Nimda", F-Secure, www.f-secure.com/v-descs/nimda.shtml#:~:text=The%20first%20variant%20in%20the,quickly%20spread%20around%20the%20world.&text=Nimda%20is%20the%20first%20worm,scan%20for%20vulnerable%20web%20sites

[73] In general, *"command and control"* (C2 aka C&C) and *"command-and-control systems"* refer to the overall concept of how organizations, particularly military, intelligence, and government forces, exercise authority and coordinate their activities. Typically *"command and control center"* (C&C) refers to a physical location, such as a facility, server, or system where command and control operations are conducted. While there is some overlap between the terms, *"command and control,"* *"C2,"* and *"C&C"* may have slightly different connotations depending on the context in which they are used.

[74] The information security, cybersecurity, and Digital Forensics and Incident Response industries just love their acronyms, and I recognize that there are all sorts of industry terms related to endpoint detection and response (EDR), including managed detection and response (MDR) which is EDR + a monitoring team. There is also extended detection and response (XDR), which takes EDR and adds telemetry from nontraditional information technology (IT) endpoints, such as networking equipment, cloud applications, etc. There is also next generation antivirus (NGAV), which can be bundled with any of the aforementioned, but is intended to build upon traditional signature-based detection and augment with behavior-based detection and machine learning with a healthy dose of marketing buzzwords.

of what antivirus started out as, i.e., identify threats, protect the user, and reduce risk to data. EDR has evolved to allow for the monitoring and capture of tactics, techniques, and procedures (TTP) so security operations center (SOC) teams can detect and/or look for the *"footprints"*[75] of threat actors within networks through understanding the totality of maliciousness and suspiciousness of the The Kroll Intrusion Lifecycle™ and not just the binary presence of their malicious tools.

If you are or were a Harry Potter fan, EDR may sound a lot like Harry's "marauders' map". Modern EDR does share uncanny similarities to what the National Library of Scotland so aptly describes as "...the map [that] includes every hallway, secret passage, and classroom. In addition, it also shows the exact location of every person within the castle and its grounds, even the ghosts."

---

75 The marauders' map. National Library of Scotland. www.nls.uk/exhibitions/maps/map-of-the-month/december

THE CONSTANCY OF THE CRIMINAL MINDSET

From my years of working Incident Response investigations, I can tell you that just like traditional street criminals, cyber threat actors largely learn from crimes they commit. They consciously or unconsciously develop their patterns, preferences, and cadence just like investigators do in the detection, protection, and response to criminal acts. The most successful will document or automate their activities to *"rinse and repeat"* more easily. In fact, threat actors often cast themselves as faux business professionals, replicating their methodology with each victim they target to even include and offer *"penetration testing"* results of how they conducted their attack to *"educate the victim."*

This behavioral constancy drove me in 2022 to document and develop **The Kroll Intrusion Lifecycle™** [76]. Initially, I wanted to help Kroll's Global Consulting business visually convey to clients, lawyers, and cyber insurance professionals the most common order of operations in which threat actors and intruders could traverse a victim's proverbial *"castle"*[77]. It is intended to lay out a visual style and narrative, breaking down the technical steps and helping clients connect the dots of what happened in their incident, the fundamental facts with interwoven opinions and conclusions, while navigating from the storyteller's perspective. Beyond enabling insight and clarity, my model supports better-informed security decision-making. It was also designed to allow for overlay and natural cross-compatibility with existing and in-depth frameworks, such as MITRE ATT&CK®.

---

[76] www.kroll.com/en/insights/publications/cyber/kroll-intrusion-lifecycle
[77] Chapter 7 covers this analogy much more in depth.

As I worked through several drafts, I incorporated the knowledge and experience gained from nearly two decades and personal visibility across thousands of investigations. This led to creating a standardized approach that quantifies the behavioral elements of the lifecycle — beginning, middle and end — and specifies each stage of the intrusion threat sequence in simple, easy-to-understand terms and a visual framework.

The Kroll Intrusion Lifecycle™ has proved very successful in enabling diverse stakeholders, from executive leadership to insurance claims managers to attorneys, to track, understand, and themselves then explain the stages of modern attacks. Because the overarching actor behavior is so consistent, the framework has been relevant for an equally wide variety of purposes:

- Corporate leadership teams have benefited by having a better grasp of how their businesses suffered supply chain attacks, including how the threat actors maintained persistence and exfiltrated data.
- Pre-briefings to attorneys at regional and global law firms help educate and arm them with understanding the gravity of data extortion incidents so they can more effectively educate their clients on technical concepts and prepare for notification to third parties as required by state and regulatory laws.
- Fortune 500 corporate Incident Response teams gain a clearer vision of the multi-stage strategies that nation-state and organized crime threat actor groups employ.
- Insurance and broker professionals can walk through real-world investigations to educate and train the next generation of claims adjusters and insurance sales workforces.

Similarly, the model applies to the entire spectrum of attacker missions: from a business email compromise (BEC) to a network intrusion resulting in data exfiltration and/or ransomware to an insider threat[78]. Kroll's lifecycle model works to explain and visually describe adversarial actions regardless of whether the attacker is a **lone wolf**, an **organized crime group**, or a **nation state-sponsored advanced persistent threat** (APT) group.

In the context of cybersecurity and cybercrime, a **lone wolf** threat actor is traditionally an individual who operates independently, without being affiliated with any specific organized crime group or advanced persistent threat (APT) group. To counterbalance this broad statement, I have observed threat actors leverage ransomware from multiple groups and others who have openly admitted during negotiations and direct communications that they are freelancers and sell to the highest bidders. I characterize this category of individuals typically as possessing the skills and knowledge to carry out various cyberattacks, such as direct system exploitation, access brokering, malware distribution, or social engineering campaigns. Lone wolf threat actors can be categorized based on various factors, including their **motivations**. Their motivation can range from financial gain to political or ideological beliefs. Some may be hacktivists fighting for a cause, while others may seek personal notoriety or revenge. I have worked investigations against lone wolf operators looking to do nothing more than get rich, while others have been looking for a platform to espouse their beliefs, political being the most common.

The second characteristic is **skill level**. Lone wolf threat actors can have varying levels of expertise, from novice *"I-Can-Only-Follow-The-Playbook"* to

---

[78] Discussed more in depth in Chapter 10.

highly skilled professionals with years of experience in overcoming system and network security layers.

The third characteristic is categorical **targeting**. I have suspected that a range of lone wolf actors over the years target their victims opportunistically and once they successfully gain unauthorized access, are more likely to harass the victim and dwell because time is on their side.. The choice of target can be influenced by the actor's motivation, skill level, and opportunity.

Tactics, techniques, and procedures (TTPs) is a fourth characteristic. The methods used by lone wolf threat actors can vary greatly. I have observed off-the-shelf tools, creation and packaging of custom malware, or leveraging social engineering to infiltrate systems and networks. It is important to note that lone wolf threat actors can be more difficult to detect and attribute than organized crime groups or APTs because they tend to have wildcard characteristics in their tactics. I once had an investigation in which the combination of tooling matched another similar extortion and stalking investigation and we just outright asked the threat actor during negotiations if they were aware of a specific domain and there was a moment of almost comedic bragging in which the threat actor started bragging and then realized that the only way we could have known was if we were the same investigative team.

THE KROLL INTRUSION LIFECYCLE™ - STAGE BY STAGE

The Kroll Intrusion Lifecycle™ illustrates how attacks follow a clear behavioral sequence of distinct stages.

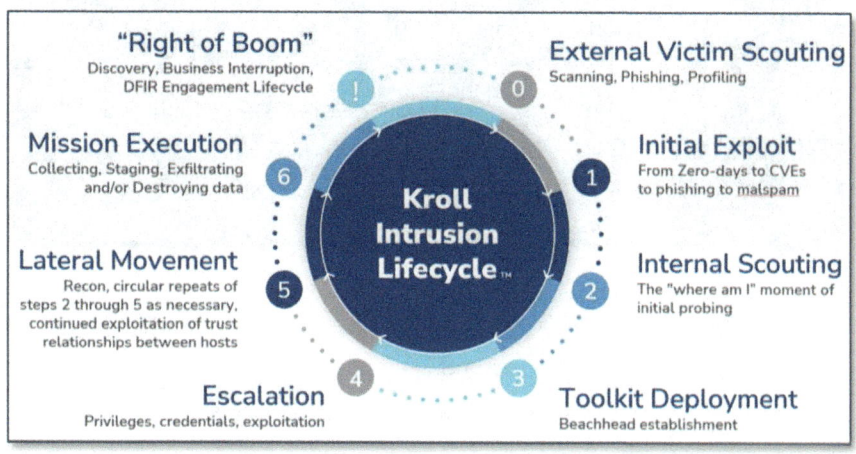

STAGE 0 - EXTERNAL VICTIM SCOUTING

Nearly all intrusions involve some type of scouting stage, although attackers may not have specific targets in mind when they start. This is the stage where the attacker may collect information about a victim through the review or scanning of external-facing infrastructure, email account passwords, social media profiles, previously dumped passwords of employees, or any other resources they can find or purchase. Their techniques may be automated through scanning, undertaken manually through collections, or purchased through dark net or deep web marketplaces. This stage may also be more passive and involve paid search result ad-positioning as covered in Chapter 9 discussing BlackCat's techniques and related-watering hole attacks as discussed throughout this book, to include Turla in Chapter 6.

Rather than targeting specific companies, a threat actor will often have an exploit they can leverage and will scan the internet for organizations and their internet-accessible environments which could be vulnerable and responsive to that exploit — this tactic was pushed to the top of national headlines in

May and June 2023 when the threat actor group Clop[79] leveraged zero-day attacks against MOVEit File Transfer Appliances (FTA). From there, they can automate what is identified in **The Kroll Intrusion Lifecycle™** as the initial chain for moving from External Victim Scouting to Initial Exploit/Actor Foothold and seeing which organizations they are able to compromise for a further attack. The actor has identified the proverbial house to target, gained intelligence about the house from what they can "*see*" at a distance, and is now preparing to act.

---

[79] Further discussed in Chapter 6.

STAGE 1 - INITIAL EXPLOIT/ACTOR FOOTHOLD

Regardless of the chosen initial intrusion vector, the goal for the threat actor remains the same: to gain and maintain a foothold within a victim's environment (the house). Whatever the exercise or intention, there is always some level of initial exploitation. This varies widely and can include, but is not limited to, zero-day vulnerabilities, unpatched CVE exploits, phishing for credentials, upstream supply chain attacks, purchasing previously gained footholds from initial access brokers, etc. The actor has now moved from outside of the house (perimeter defenses or networking hardware) to the inside.

STAGE 2 - INTERNAL VICTIM SCOUTING

This is the "*where am I moment?*" for the threat actor when they are scanning for internal IP addresses and host names, mapping Active Directory[80] object relationships and accessible network shares [81], identifying naming conventions, etc. At this stage, the attacker is exploring options and inventorying paths in order to identify how to reach their next objective. They are becoming oriented and assessing the position in the network or system that Stage 1 took them to. This stage is sometimes limited by the nature of the computer system or by domain account role/permissions they have initial access to. The actor has arrived in a location they have not likely been before and are quickly searching for where to go next. This is the stage where the threat actor may not fully understand the environment they are in, so they may log into servers or push malware across the network to computers that later, from a forensics perspective, do not make sense in the intrusion lifecycle, but at the time, were simply an exploratory step by the threat actor.

I recall one investigation that I was working and our team had pieced together a timeline enough to be able to inform the victim that the threat actor had moved laterally in their network among three systems, but then had

---

[80] Active Directory (AD) is a directory service developed by Microsoft for use in Windows domain networks. It is a centralized database that stores information about objects on a network, including user accounts, computer accounts, and resources such as printers and servers. AD provides a single point of management for network resources, allowing administrators to manage user accounts and access permissions across multiple computers and servers in a domain. It also provides security features such as authentication and authorization, which allow users to access only the resources they are authorized to use. AD uses a hierarchical structure, with domains as the primary unit of organization. Domains can be grouped into forests, which represent a collection of one or more domains that share a common schema, configuration, and global catalog. Active Directory can be used to manage and secure various aspects of a Windows network, including user authentication, group policies, security permissions, and application deployment.
[81] Network shares are locations where storage exists in another place, but your computer has a path to that as if it was a local drive or volume. Think Google Drive, Drop Box, One Drive, etc., where the files are accessible, openable, and searchable, but more specific to being inside of a corporate network and you have a drive letter where you store files so that others can easily access them also.

immediately logged off them. When I asked what the role of the servers were, the client confirmed that they had been testing a new endpoint detection and response tool on the three systems, but had not yet purchased the licenses for full enterprise rollout. The lightbulb moment for our team was that the threat actor must have logged in, observed the security software running, and immediately logged out so as to minimize detection. As our team dug in further, we noticed that the threat actors had also identified the SCCM[82] server within the network, had logged in, inventoried all of the whitelisted deployment packages and, in our assessment, had learned which software they could leverage within the network to "*live off the land*" without bringing additional, noisy malware or third-party software into the network. Ultimately, the threat actor leveraged authorized file transfer software to exfiltrate data and took advantage of authorized remote access tooling used by the internal information technology team to install and move around the environment, hiding in plain sight.

---

[82] SCCM stands for System Center Configuration Manager and is a software management suite provided by Microsoft that allows users to manage a large number of Windows-based computers. SCCM features remote control, patch management, operating system deployment, network protection, and other various services. An SCCM server refers to the server system on which the SCCM software is installed. This server communicates with client computers and executes administrative tasks, such as deploying software, applying updates, or configuring settings on those client computers.

STAGE 3 - TOOLKIT DEPLOYMENT

At this point, the threat actor makes the decision to launch forward and choose the tools they need to achieve their goal based on Stage 2 scouting results. They may implant persistence mechanisms, backdoor methods for additional remote access to the network, and enable communications with external command-and-control (C2) servers. This will allow them to install malicious tools, push/pull remote commands, increase their reach within the network, escalate privileges, and monitor endpoints — anything that can enable them to implement their attack. Typically, my forensic teams have observed threat actors utilizing password stealers, freely downloadable remote access tools, and other software that allow for collection of credentials from networked computers and broadening of their lateral movement capabilities.

A good example of malware that threat actors may deploy during this stage to advance the intrusion lifecycle was documented in 2021 when I co-authored with Josh Mitchell a technical deep dive into a piece of PowerShell-based malware that we codenamed EPHEMERAL LOCKPICKER[83]. The malware was defined by four distinct features (which the linked article in the footnote dives further into), but two of the four key features relevant to this section of the chapter were that the malware was designed to make a concerted effort to remain resident only in memory and possessed unique data collection utilities for exfiltration of data, most all of which was enabled through PowerShell — an innately available capability of modern Windows operating systems as prior discussed in this book so far.

This is the stage that increases the difficulty of meaningful actor ejection and the one at which the MITRE ATT&CK[84] framework gives hundreds of indicators of compromise and tactics, techniques, and procedures (Stages 3, 4, and 5). At this stage, the threat actors are noisier, and the likelihood of detection is increasing with every moment and upon every tool execution. They are disturbing the proverbial contents and furniture of the rooms of the home they are moving through.

---

[83] Ackerman, D. & Mitchell, J. (2021). "EPHEMERAL LOCKPICKER: Malware Leveraged for Novel Intrusion Lifecycle and LuckyDay Ransomware Delivery". Kroll. www.kroll.com/en/insights/publications/cyber/ephemeral-lockpicker-malware-novel-intrusion-lifecycle

[84] https://attack.mitre.org

STAGE 4 - ESCALATION

The threat actor uses their tools and pilfered credentials to escalate from lower privileges to higher privileges and not only increase their reach within the victim's environment, but move from less sensitive systems to more sensitive internal systems or resouces. This is because, even with tools, an attacker at Stage 3 does not typically have broad network access, but they are gaining it. While I have observed network intruders that go from internal scouting straight to execution of mission in hours, sometimes due to dumb luck, sometimes due to expertise of craft or initial exploitation, most of the time I observe that an actor has entered with a lower set of privileges and access and then leveraged tooling to gain or increase their level of access within the environment. Having escalated roles and privileges gives the actor more "*access rights*" to move on to the next stage.

STAGE 5 - LATERAL MOVEMENT/RECONNAISSANCE

If necessary, the attack involves the cyclical repetition of Stages 2 to 5, but continues the exploitation of trust relationships between machines and networks (e.g., rooms within the house) to expand and deepen the network intrusion to other target computers or portions of the network. This is usually the stage of lateral movement with the goal of accessing the destination of valuable or sensitive data holdings. The attacker now needs to go to where their target is. Typically, in an intrusion lifecycle, threat actors gain access on an external-facing system through an exploit, an externally facing login capability, or through the victim's virtual private network (VPN). From there, their aim is to reach the domain controller for purposes of broader privileged access escalation through account identification and credential theft to broaden their reach within the domain. From there, they are looking for systems of value – this stage of the lifecycle – typically file storage servers or network attached storage (NAS) devices with large volumes of files and folders containing sensitive data.

STAGE 6 - EXECUTION OF MISSION

The final stage of the intrusion lifecycle is where the attacker achieves their ultimate objective – their end goal – whether that is collecting, staging, exfiltrating, and/or destroying data. Once they have achieved their objective, the intrusion lifecycle is fundamentally over. The attacker moves on to their next victim and repeats the intrusion lifecycle all over again, starting from Stage 0.

```
01010100 01101000 01100101 01110010 01100101 00100000 01100001 01110010 01100101
00100000 00110001 00110000 00100000 01110100 01111001 01110000 01100101 01110011
00100000 01101111 01100110 00100000 01110000 01100101 01101111 01110000 01101100
01100101 00111010 00100000 01110100 01101000 01101111 01110011 01100101 00100000
01110111 01101000 01101111 00100000 01110101 01101110 01100100 01100101 01110010
01110011 01110100 01100001 01101110 01100100 00100000 01100010 01101001 01101110
01100001 01110010 01111001 00101100 00100000 01100001 01101110 01100100 00100000
01110100 01101000 01101111 01110011 01100101 00100000 01110111 01101000 01101111
00100000 01100100 01101111 01101110 1000000011001 01110100 00101110
```

CHAPTER 6 - THE TRICKLE DOWN EFFECT

For many years now, after investigating the aftermath left behind by organized crime groups, I and my investigative teams have witnessed how these groups adapt, adopt, and mirror APTs in their tactics and techniques, specifically in targeted attacks against victims. This is what I refer to the *"Trickle Down Effect"* during my *"Threats, Trends, and Tactics"* keynote talks. This chapter explores what I have observed and documented [85] regarding organized cybercrime groups learning from APTs and what corporate executives can do to protect their organizations against these evolving threats.

---

[85] A professional colleague and personal friend, whom I greatly respect, and I were conversing once, and I was attempting to make a play on words with a particular phrase from the then popular HBO Game of Thrones TV show - *"That's what I do, I drink and I know things,"* but I said *"I know a thing or two, about a thing or two"* – we had a good laugh, but it stuck. We still joke about it to this day.

STUDYING APT TACTICS AND TECHNIQUES

Advanced persistent threat (APT) actor groups are nation-state-sponsored and as you might imagine, have access to more extensive resources, training, and capabilities compared to their private sector and organized crime *"cousins."* They typically conduct sophisticated attacks against specific targets over longer than average periods of time, focusing on goals that ultimately benefit their sponsoring nation state. Most often, we see these groups attempting to acquire research, technology, information, and/or intelligence that will give their sponsors economic, scientific, and/or military advantages. These groups often rely on tactics such as social engineering, spear-phishing, and zero-day exploits to gain access to their targets' networks and quietly work in the background for as long as their mission takes. Operations can last from months to years.

Organized cybercrime groups, on the other hand, are typically profit-driven and operate on a smaller, less organized scale than APTs. However, they have recognized the value of learning from APTs in order to improve their capabilities and toolsets and increase their operational chances of success. One way in which organized cybercrime groups learn from APTs is by studying their tactics and techniques, gaining insights into how to conduct more effective and targeted attacks of their own. The tactics and techniques employed by numerous APT groups are often noteworthy because there are aspects of their attacks that are more novel or advanced than those leveraged by typical cybercriminals. In addition to studying APT tactics, cybercriminals adopt similar tools and infrastructure.

So how does this play out in real life? Let's consider the May 2017 WannaCry ransomware attacks that wreaked havoc on hundreds of thousands of computers worldwide[86]. The attacks were executed by the Lazarus Group, a notorious APT believed to be affiliated with North Korea[87]. Lazarus Group has been linked to the use of custom-built malware such as the WannaCry ransomware, which has since been used by cybercriminals in a number of high-profile attacks. The Server Message Block (SMB) exploit central to the attack was originally discovered by the U.S. National Security Agency, and subsequently leaked by hackers. The following graphic shows what I propose is the Trickle Down Effect from nation state to organized crime groups:

---

[86] The US and UK governments pointed direct political fingers at North Korea for the WannaCry malware attack. The attack was assessed in open sources as having affected more than 300,000 computers across 150 countries, causing billions of dollars of estimated damage. The US indicted three North Koreans for the WannaCry malware and the 2014 Sony Pictures Entertainment hack. The US specifically named Park Jin Hyok, a 34-year-old North Korean, as one of many involved individuals.

[87] U.S. Department of Justice. (n.d.). North Korean Regime-Backed Programmer Charged With Conspiracy to Conduct Multiple Cyber Attacks and Intrusions. www.justice.gov/opa/pr/north-korean-regime-backed-programmer-charged-conspiracy-conduct-multiple-cyber-attacks-and

WannaCry ransomware first appeared in May 2017. It was designed to spread rapidly across computer networks, encrypting files on infected computers and demanding payment in exchange for a decryption key to unlock the files. The ransomware affected well over 200,000 computers across more than 150 countries, including the United Kingdom's National Health Service (NHS), which was forced to cancel appointments and divert patients to other hospitals. WannaCry exploited a vulnerability in Microsoft Windows operating systems, which was initially discovered by the U.S. National Security Agency (NSA) and later leaked by a hacker group known as Shadow Brokers. The ransomware was designed to spread rapidly across networks because it used a worm-like capability to self-replicate and infect other computers that were not properly patched or updated with security patches. The WannaCry attackers demanded payment in the form of bitcoin. However, many victims refused to pay the ransom, and a security researcher was able to identify and activate a web domain-associated "kill switch" that stopped the spread of the malware upon a preprogrammed check in. Despite this, WannaCry caused significant disruption and financial losses for many organizations, and it served as a warning about the potential impact of ransomware attacks on critical infrastructure and services.

ADOPTING SIMILAR TOOLS AND INFRASTRUCTURE

APT groups often use custom-built malware and other tools that are designed to evade detection and bypass security measures. When I have the opportunity to study their tactics and interpret their left-behind malware or intrusion marks through the skillsets of my global teams, I am effectively taking the steps that cybercriminals are also taking. Whereas I am investigating a victim to make them whole again, cybercriminals are reading blogs from security practitioners, watching security talks online from conferences, reading malware teardowns from malware reverse engineers, and pulling down malware from VirusTotal like the rest of us within the cybersecurity and Digital Forensics and Incident Response industries. One side is educating and learning, and so is the other.

By acquiring or creating similar tools, cybercriminals improve their ability to carry out successful attacks. Even acknowledging the fact that APT groups have access to greater resources, training, capabilities, and infrastructure by their very nature of being associated with government budgets and military complexes, the skills gap has closed in recent years. This is especially apparent with the blurring of lines between true APT group members and those same actors who are suspected of moonlighting for organized criminal groups for financial gain on the side – the literal *"Trickle Down Effect"* with the transfer of APT level knowledge to organized crime groups directly.

BUT WHY DO THEY DO IT?

While conducting research for this chapter, one of the things that I focused on was the economic factors behind monthly and annual salaries for white- and blue-collar workers across Eastern European countries. According to available data from research resources that included tradingeconomics.com and russialounge.com, some interesting and noteworthy numbers emerged:

- The average monthly salaries for a white-collar worker in Russia was approximately 97,000 RUB (approximately USD1,197) and the average monthly salary for a blue-collar worker was 47,000 RUB (approximately USD580) as of June 2023[88].
- In Ukraine, the average monthly salary for a white-collar worker was 14,000 UAH (approximately USD377) and the average monthly salary for a blue-collar worker was 10,000 UAH (approximately USD269) as of June 2023.

Understanding the financial landscape of Russia was crucial to comprehending why certain organized crime groups choose the paths they do and why they seem to be based out of the regions of the world that they are. Ransomware payments can net them hundreds of thousands or millions of US dollars in weeks or months' worth of *"work"* compared to mainstream options within their communities or countries of citizenship. The comparison to the average monthly or annual salaries emerged as the telltale signs of why *"crime pays"* in certain regions of the world more so than others.

It was also telling that certain online Russian and Eastern European communities and forums largely argued opinions that salary averages reported by the government, western civilization news agencies, and

---

[88] Trading Economics. Russia - Wages. https://tradingeconomics.com/russia/wages

independent salary comparison websites did not account for the large number of Russians participating in the **shadow** or **informal economy**[89] which involved an estimated one-fifth of Russia's workforce who did not pay taxes and did not appear in official statistics. The Russian **shadow** or **informal economy** refers to economic activities that are not regulated by the government and are not included in official statistics. The size of Russia's informal economy is indeed significant and is estimated to be 38% of the country's GDP at Purchasing Power Parity (PPP) levels, which represents approximately $1,518 billion USD[90]. As for comparisons with other countries, a report from World Economics shows that Russia's informal economy **size is only slightly larger than that of Senegal**, which is at 37.7%[91]. Why the comparison? As of 2020, Russia had a GDP per capita of $26,500 USD while Senegal's was $3,300 USD. Senegal is 87 times smaller than Russia! Senegal had a population of approximately 17 million compared to Russia had a population of nearly 147 million. Interesting in my humble opinion.

The main components of the Russian shadow economy are envelope wages (wages paid under the table) and underreporting of business profits, with the former being approximately 38.7% of the true wage and the latter being approximately 33.8% of actual business income. Unregistered companies, which are completely off the books, make up about 6.1% of all enterprises in Russia. A high level of bribery is another notable component of the shadow economy in Russia, with the magnitude of bribery (percentage of revenue

---

[89] "Russia Lounge." (2019, August 4). The Normal Russian Salary. Russia Lounge. https://russialounge.com/normal-russian-salary
[90] World Economics. Russia: Informal Economy. www.worldeconomics.com/Informal-Economy/Russia.aspx
[91] FREE NETWORK. (2020, March 16). The Shadow Economy in Russia: New Estimates and Comparisons with Nearby Countries. https://freepolicybriefs.org/2020/03/16/shadow-economy-russia

spent on *"getting things done"*) estimated to be 26.4%[92]. The informal labor market in Russia is reported to have been shrinking, with one in three Russians currently engaged in the informal economy, down from almost 45% two years ago. This still amounts to around 25 million Russians working illegally[93]. Unregistered work is most common in the service, agriculture, and construction industries, as do those that require lower levels of education.

Let's round out the research with surrounding Eastern European countries such as Poland and Hungary. The average monthly salary for a white-collar worker was higher than that of Russia and Ukraine.

- In Poland, the average monthly salary for a white-collar worker was 5,200 PLN (approximately $1,400 USD) and for blue-collar workers, the average monthly salary was 3,600 PLN (approximately $970 USD) as of June 2023.
- In Hungary, the average monthly salary for a white-collar worker was 391,000 HUF (approximately $1,300 USD) and for blue-collar workers, the average monthly salary was 242,000 HUF (approximately $800 USD) as of June 2023.

Table 1 shows the global disparity in wages as of July 2023 and how they are likely driving threat actor activity.

---

[92] World Economics. Shadow Economy Size www.worldeconomics.com/Informal-Economy
[93] The Moscow Times. (2019, October 29). How Big Is Russia's Shadow Economy and Why Does It Matter? www.themoscowtimes.com/2019/10/29/big-russias-shadow-informal-economy-matter-a67817

Table 1 – Mid Level White Collar Salaries 2023

Country[94]	Average Salary (USD)[95]	Average Salary (USD)
USA (white collar)	$57,256/year	$2,385/month
USA (blue collar)	$52,901/year	$2,204/month
Germany	$54,840/year	$2,285/month
Slovakia	$31,440/year	$1,310/month
Russia	$14,771/year	$615/month
Belarus	$8,004/year	$333/month
Czech Republic	$8,772/year	$365/month

---

[94] Time Doctor. (2023, June). What is the average salary in Russia? www.timedoctor.com
[95] ZipRecruiter. (2023, May). Salary: Mid Level White Collar. www.ziprecruiter.com

BLURRING LINES BETWEEN APT & ORGANIZED CRIMINAL GROUPS

Advanced persistent threat (APT) groups are often associated with state-sponsored cyber espionage and are known for their great levels of sophisticated and often, targeted attacks. However, there is a growing trend of suspected and confirmed former APT members being recruited by or moonlighting for organized crime groups to carry out financially motivated cyberattacks. This dangerous alliance has serious implications for global cybersecurity in that well financed, well recruited, well funded skills of former (or current) APT members can be harnessed by organized crime groups for goals that range from financial profit to the destabilization of national infrastructure or industry sectors.

TURLA

To see what organizations are up against, let us consider the Turla APT group and the advanced attack capabilities one of its members can bring to an organized crime group. Also known as Snake or Uroburos, Turla has been active since at least 2007 and is suspected in numerous open- and closed-source reports to have strong links to the Russian government. Reports have tied Turla to Russia's domestic intelligence and security service FSB [96], specifically with cyberattacks on Ukrainian technical infrastructure. Turla is known for its cyber-espionage campaigns and targeted attacks against government, diplomatic, and military organizations worldwide.

---

[96] The Russian FSB (Federal Security Service) is the main domestic security agency of the Russian Federation, and is responsible for the country's internal security, counterintelligence, and border control. It was established in 1995, following the breakup of the Soviet Union and the dissolution of the KGB. The FSB is considered to be one of the successor agencies to the KGB, and it is responsible for collecting and analyzing intelligence, conducting counterterrorism operations, and monitoring political dissent and opposition to the government. The FSB is also involved in cybersecurity and counterespionage activities and has been linked to various cyberattacks and hacking campaigns targeting foreign governments, businesses, and individuals.

Turla has employed a variety of techniques to infiltrate, compromise, and maintain access to target networks over the years. Some of the key technical aspects of their hacking strategies include the following (as you read through this list, again, consider the possible ways they could be used against your organization and how you might detect, contain, and counter):

- **Custom Malware**: Turla is known for developing and using custom malware in their operations, such as the Snake rootkit, which has enabled them to gain and maintain persistence in a compromised system. The Snake rootkit was designed to hide its presence and communication with its command-and-control (C2) servers, making it conceivably above average in difficulty to detect and analyze.

- **Watering Hole Attacks:** Turla has been observed using watering hole attacks [97], where they compromise legitimate websites by injecting malicious code that runs upon being visited. The websites are picked and compromised as they are frequently visited by their intended targets. When a target visits the compromised site, the code exploits vulnerabilities in their system to deliver Turla's malware, allowing for The Kroll Intrusion Lifecycle™ to kick off at Stage 1.

- **Spear-Phishing:** Turla also relies on spear-phishing emails to deliver their malware. These emails are highly targeted and tailored to the specific interests of the recipient, often appearing to come

---

[97] A watering hole attack is a type of cyberattack that can target specific groups of users by infecting a website that is known to be frequently visited. The attackers compromise the website by injecting malicious code, which can then infect the computers of visitors to the site with malware. The goal of a watering hole attack is to gain access to sensitive information or systems belonging to the targeted group of users or organizations, but by nature of this style attack, typically a broad range of victims are affected, and the threat actor needs to conduct research into identifying the focused set of victims of interest. This type of attack is often used by hackers to gain access to networks and data belonging to government agencies, corporations, or other high-value targets.

from a trusted source. The emails[98] contain malicious attachments or links that, when opened, are intended to infect the target's system with Turla's malware with a high rate of success.

- **Lateral Movement:** Once inside a target's network, Turla employs lateral movement techniques to gain access to additional systems and resources. The group has traditionally been observed leveraging tooling such as PowerShell and Mimikatz to escalate privileges, harvest credentials, and move laterally within the network.

---

[98] Sayegh, E. (2023, March 8). Turla hacking group: A persistent international threat. Forbes. www.forbes.com/sites/emilsayegh/2023/03/07/turla-hacking-group-a-persistent-international-threat/?sh=3b7a092a7498

NOTABLE HACKING & BIG GAME HUNTING STORIES

- **European Government Network Compromise:** In 2018, Turla was linked to a significant breach of a European government's secure network. The attackers managed to maintain persistence within the network for over a year, exfiltrating sensitive data and intelligence. Turla used a combination of spear-phishing, custom malware, and lateral movement techniques to carry out the attack.

- **Gazer:** In 2017, researchers discovered a previously unknown Turla backdoor called Gazer, which had been used to compromise diplomatic and government organizations across Europe and the Middle East. Gazer utilized a sophisticated and modular infrastructure to maintain persistence in compromised networks, enabling the attackers to conduct long-term espionage operations. The backdoor was delivered through spear-phishing emails and watering hole attacks and leveraged encrypted C2 communication to evade detection[99].

- **Satellite-based C2 Communications:** Turla was found to have been capable of leveraging satellite-based C2 communications to hide their tracks and maintain a covert presence in their targets' networks. By leveraging satellite-based internet service providers, Turla was able to obfuscate the location of their origin C2 servers and avoid detection. This innovative technique demonstrated the group's advanced technical capabilities and their determination to

---

[99] Gazer: A new backdoor targets ministries and embassies worldwide. The Hacker News. (2017, August 30). https://thehackernews.com/2017/08/gazer-backdoor-malware.html

remain hidden while traversing and moving through compromised networks[100].

- **LightNeuron:** In 2019, researchers discovered a sophisticated Turla backdoor called LightNeuron [101], which targeted Microsoft Exchange servers. LightNeuron was specifically designed to intercept and manipulate emails, enabling the attackers to exfiltrate sensitive information, inject malicious code into legitimate email threads, and send spear-phishing emails from compromised, but legitimate email accounts which increase the likelihood of downstream attack successes. The malware's complex architecture and stealthy communication mechanisms made it challenging to detect and analyze[102].

- **Kopiluwak and QuietCanary:** In 2022, researchers documented an incredibly novel approach to hiding in plain sight. Researchers found that the reconnaissance utility Kopiluwak [103] was downloaded through the presence of another commodity banking Trojan known

---

[100] Drozhzhin, A., Ilyin, Y., Team, K., Kaminsky, S., & Titterington, A. (2015, September 9). Russian-speaking cyber spies from Turla APT Group exploit satellites. Daily English Global blogkasperskycom. www.kaspersky.com/blog/turla-apt-exploiting-satellites/9771

[101] LightNeuron was a relatively sophisticated backdoor malware that targeted Microsoft Exchange email servers, allowing attackers to perform various malicious activities such as stealing sensitive information, executing arbitrary commands, and intercepting and forwarding emails. LightNeuron was unique in that it was designed to be integrated directly into the Exchange transport agent, which was responsible for handling incoming and outgoing email messages. This allowed the malware to intercept and manipulate email messages at a very low level, making it difficult to detect and defend against. The LightNeuron malware could be controlled remotely through a specially crafted email message, which contained encoded commands that were executed by the malware when the message was processed by the Exchange server. This made it possible for attackers to maintain persistent control over the compromised Exchange server and exfiltrate sensitive data over a long period of time.

[102] Higgins, K. J. (2019, May 7). Russian Nation-State Group Employs Custom Backdoor for Microsoft Exchange Server. Dark Reading. www.darkreading.com/application-security/russian-nation-state-group-employs-custom-backdoor-for-microsoft-exchange-server

[103] Kopiluwak is primarily a reconnaissance tool, capable of collecting system information including OS version, installed software, and other system details, executing arbitrary commands, data exfiltration capabilities over command-and-control (C2) traffic, and persistence capabilities including scheduled tasks and registry keys.

as Andromeda. Deeper analysis and forensics tracked the presence of a second piece of malware dubbed QuietCanary[104] that identified, targeted, captured, and exfiltrated target data. According to the researchers, this was an exclusive hallmark and tactical move of Turla. Review of the C2 servers for the Andromeda malware sourced back to web domains that had expired and been re-registered in 2022 after having gone dormant. Additional domain name recognition and parallel IP address analysis revealed additional expired and re-registered domains, as if a threat actor had decided to hide in the noise of a global commodity malware's wake and silently hijack infrastructure for different tactics and spying. This tactic is brilliant in that you hide in the noise, like a spy simply walking down the street of a busy city in the middle of a beautiful spring day — normal, expected, and just another person walking through their day.

---

[104] Hall, R., & Sadowski, J. (2022, March 4). Responses to Russia's invasion of Ukraine likely to spur retaliation. Mandiant. www.mandiant.com/resources/blog/russia-invasion-ukraine-retaliation

LAZARUS GROUP

The Lazarus Group is an APT group with reported connections to the North Korean government and has been implicated in several high-profile cyberattacks, such as the Sony Pictures hack in 2014 and the WannaCry ransomware outbreak heard *"around the world"* of 2017[105]. However, former members of the Lazarus Group have been linked to financially motivated cybercrime, such as the 2016 Bangladesh Bank heist[106], which resulted in the theft of $81 million. The Lazarus Group's focus on cryptocurrency money laundering and related thefts is covered further in Chapter 9.

The Lazarus Group employs a wide range of techniques to infiltrate, compromise, and maintain access to their targets' networks. Some of their key technical strategies include:

---

[105] Zahorski, A. (2022, July 10). What Is the Lazarus Group? Is It Really Comprised of North Korean Hackers? MUO. www.makeuseof.com/what-is-the-lazarus-group
[106] Lema, K. (March 29, 2017,). Bangladesh bank heist was 'state-sponsored': U.S. official. Reuters. www.reuters.com/article/us-cyber-heist-philippines/bangladesh-bank-heist-was-state-sponsored-u-s-official-idUSKBN1700TI

- **Custom Malware:** The Lazarus Group is known for developing and using custom malware in their operations, such as WannaCry ransomware, which caused a global outbreak in 2017, and the Destover[107] wiper malware used in the 2014 Sony Pictures hack. Sophisticated tools like these enable the group to effectively compromise systems, maintain persistence, and exfiltrate or destroy data.

- **Spear-Phishing:** The group relies heavily on spear-phishing emails, which are highly targeted and tailored to the recipient's interests, often appearing to originate from a trusted source. These emails contain malicious attachments or links that, when opened, infect the target's system with Lazarus Group's malware.

- **Supply Chain Attacks:** Lazarus has also been known to use supply chain attacks, where they have compromised third-party software or service providers to deliver their malware to a broader range of targets. One example is the 2018 compromise of a cryptocurrency exchange platform's software update mechanism, which allowed Lazarus to distribute their malware to users who downloaded the update[108]. Another example is the alleged 2023 compromise of enterprise communications services provider 3CX[109], assessed via open source as having been initiated itself via a user that downloaded

---

[107] The primary objective of Destover in this attack was to delete files and overwrite the Master Boot Record (MBR) of affected machines, rendering them inoperable and causing significant damage to the company's IT infrastructure. Destover's destructive nature and its association with the Sony Pictures attack make it a significant example of a targeted, politically motivated cyberattack.

[108] Park, J. (2021). The Lazarus Group: The Cybercrime Syndicate Financing the North Korea State. Harvard International Review, 42(2). https://hir.harvard.edu/the-cybercrime-syndicate-financing-the-north-korean-state

[109] Johnson, J., Plan, F., Sanchez, A., Fontana, R., & Nicastro, J. (n.d.). 3CX software supply chain compromise initiated by a prior software supply chain compromise; suspected North Korean actor responsible. Mandiant. www.mandiant.com/resources/blog/3cx-software-supply-chain-compromise

a trojanized version of a trading software application for their personal use on a 3CX endpoint[110], resulting in one of the first documented double supply chain attacks per Mandiant's Incident Response team.

- **Lateral Movement:** Once inside a target's network, the Lazarus Group has been observed employing tools such as PowerShell and Mimikatz to escalate privileges, harvest credentials, and move laterally within the network[111].

Several factors suggest that the Lazarus Group has strong connections to the North Korean government:

- **Target Selection:** The Lazarus Group's targets often align with North Korea's geopolitical interests, including foreign governments, media organizations, and financial institutions[112].

- **Language and Infrastructure:** Lazarus Group's malware and C&C infrastructure have been found to contain Korean language artifacts, and some of their attacks have been traced back to North Korean geolocated IP addresses[113].

- **Operational Hours:** Analysis of the Lazarus Group's activity has revealed that the group's operational hours align with the working

---

[110] Greenberg, A. (2023, April 20). The huge 3CX breach was actually 2 linked supply chain attacks. Wired. www.wired.com/story/3cx-supply-chain-attack-times-two
[111] Hidden Cobra – North Korea's DDOS Botnet Infrastructure: CISA. Cybersecurity and Infrastructure Security Agency CISA. (2023, April 13). www.cisa.gov/news-events/alerts/2017/06/13/hidden-cobra-north-koreas-ddos-botnet-infrastructure
[112] Federal Bureau of Investigation. (n.d.). Park Jin Hyok. FBI. www.fbi.gov/wanted/cyber/park-jin-hyok
[113] Kaspersky Lab. (2016, February 12). Operation Blockbuster: Unveiling the Long-known Secret. Kaspersky Daily. https://usa.kaspersky.com/blog/operation-blockbuster/6763

hours of the Pyongyang time zone, further suggesting a link to the North Korean government[114].

---

[114] "North Korea, cyberattacks and 'Lazarus': What we really know", AP News. Eric Talmadge, June 2, 2017, https://apnews.com/article/china-technology-ap-top-news-north-korea-international-news-1866d617303642488615b118959bc2d8

NOTABLE HACKING & BIG GAME HUNTING STORIES

- **Sony Pictures Hack (2014):** In one of their most high-profile attacks, the Lazarus Group targeted Sony Pictures Entertainment, resulting in a massive data breach that exposed sensitive company information, unreleased films, and personal data of employees[115]. The attackers used spear-phishing emails to deliver the Destover wiper malware, which wiped hard drives and rendered systems unusable. The attack was largely assessed to be in response to Sony's intended release of "*The Interview*," a comedy film depicting a plot to assassinate North Korea's leader, Kim Jong-un[116]. In the mind of this author, this may be one of the best "*on the nose*" examples of what many assume was a modern country leader ordering their government-sponsored hacking groups to lash out at a satirical extension of Hollywood and comedy over a personal spite and ego hit[117].

- **WannaCry Ransomware Outbreak (2017):** The Lazarus Group was linked to the global WannaCry ransomware outbreak that affected hundreds of thousands of computers in over 150 countries. WannaCry exploited a vulnerability in Microsoft's SMB protocol (EternalBlue[118]), encrypting files on infected systems and demanding

---

[115] "U.S. Said to Find North Korea Ordered Cyberattack on Sony", New York Times, December 18, 2014, David E. Sanger and Nicole Perlroth, www.nytimes.com/2014/12/18/world/asia/us-links-north-korea-to-sony-hacking.html

[116] Federal Bureau of Investigation. (2014, December 19). Update on Sony investigation. FBI. www.fbi.gov/news/pressrel/press-releases/update-on-sony-investigation

[117] Sanger, D. E., & Perlroth, N. (2014, December 17). U.S. said to find North Korea ordered Cyberattack on Sony. The New York Times. www.nytimes.com/2014/12/18/world/asia/us-links-north-korea-to-sony-hacking.html

[118] EternalBlue was a cyber exploit developed by the U.S. National Security Agency (NSA) that targeted Microsoft Windows operating systems. It exploited a vulnerability in the Server Message Block (SMB) protocol. This exploit was inadvertently leaked by The Shadow Brokers in 2017, leading to prolific use and varied integration in numerous pieces of malware and across significantly different profiles of cyberattacks and campaigns globally for years.

a ransom for their release. The attack caused significant disruption to critical infrastructure, including the UK's National Health Service, and resulted in millions of dollars in damages. This is a great example of what I refer to as the *Trickle Down Effect*[119] in my keynote speeches that I have given in which nation-state-developed exploits, loosed into the public domain, and absorbed by other advanced persistent groups, are retooled and leveraged for mass-scale operations, ultimately being identified and retooled further down the line by Organized Crime Groups in what later became a myriad of banking trojan releases, including TrickBot, Emotet, Qbot aka QakBot, and others.

- **Bangladesh Bank Heist (2016):** The Lazarus Group was implicated in the cyber heist of the Bangladesh Bank, which resulted in the theft of $81 million. The attackers compromised the bank's SWIFT system and sent fraudulent money transfer requests to the Federal Reserve Bank of New York. The group leveraged custom malware known as Bankshot [120], [121], which enabled them to manipulate the SWIFT system and bypass transaction validation processes.

---

[119] Read more back in Chapter 6.

[120] Bankshot was a malware implant developed and used by the Hidden Cobra threat group (also known as Lazarus Group), which is associated with the North Korean government. The Bankshot implant was delivered via malicious Word documents and designed to provide the attackers with a backdoor into a victim's system, allowing them to gain unauthorized access and steal sensitive information. Once the Bankshot malware was installed, it communicated with a C2 server controlled by the Hidden Cobra threat actors. The attackers used the connection to remotely control the victim's system, steal data, and download additional malware (payloads). The malware was designed to evade detection by security software by leveraging advanced techniques such as encryption, compression, and fileless execution.

[121] Sherstobitoff, R. (2018, July 3). Hidden Cobra Targets Turkish Financial Sector With New Bankshot Implant. McAfee Blog. www.mcafee.com/blogs/other-blogs/mcafee-labs/hidden-cobra-targets-turkish-financial-sector-new-bankshot-implant/

- **Operation Sharpshooter (2018):** In Operation Sharpshooter, the Lazarus Group targeted critical infrastructure sectors and financial institutions in multiple countries, including the United States, Europe, and Asia. The group used spear-phishing emails to deliver a custom backdoor called Rising Sun, which allowed them to exfiltrate sensitive data and execute commands on compromised systems. The operation demonstrated the group's ongoing focus on economic and industrial targets.

CLOP

As I was writing this book, the United States government was offering a $10 million reward[122] for information on the Clop (Cl0p) threat actor group.[123] This bounty came hard on the heels of the group's massive May 2023 attack on the MOVEit file transfer system[124], which as of the writing of this chapter

---

[122] "US Offers $10 Million Bounty for Info on Clop Ransomware Gang", Vlad Constantinescu, Bitdefender, June 19, 2023, www.bitdefender.com/blog/hotforsecurity/us-offers-10-million-bounty-for-info-on-clop-ransomware-gang
[123] Clop is believed to be derived from Klop, the Russian word for a blood-sucking bedbug.
[124] MOVEit is a managed file transfer software solution allowing for secure file transfer.

had reportedly affected over 140 victim organizations, compromising the personal information of 15.5 million people[125].

Clop is suspected to have affiliations with TA505, a notorious cybercrime group that has been involved in cybercrime activity for over a decade. TA505 is considered one of the largest global distributors of phishing and malware; threat intelligence teams have assessed that the group has in one form or another infiltrated the computers of approximately 8,000 companies worldwide. In recent years, Incident Response teams like mine have witnessed a significant increase in cyberattacks on corporate and government entities. These network intrusions and data exfiltration events underscore the importance of understanding the nature of these threats.

Clop emerged in the cyber landscape as a force to be reckoned with, notable for its technological sophistication and audacious targets. Originating from Russia with Russian-speaking members as far back as 2019, this organized crime group was responsible for orchestrating numerous successful cyberattacks globally. Notably, Clop targeted high-profile entities such as the British Broadcasting Corporation (BBC) and British Airways, creating a shockwave through the corporate sector.

The organized crime group's modus operandi has often revolved around a specific breed of malware, the eponymous "*Clop*" ransomware. Using this advanced digital calling card, the group would infiltrate an organization's system, exfiltrate data, encrypt valuable data, and subsequently demand a ransom for not posting the stolen data and to decrypt the victim's encrypted systems.

---

[125] "Millions affected by MOVEit mass-hacks as list of casualties continues to grow", Carly Page, TechCrunch, June 29, 2023, https://techcrunch.com/2023/06/29/millions-affected-moveit-mass-hacks

NOTABLE HACKING & BIG GAME HUNTING STORIES

One of Clop's early significant exploits leveraged the multiple zero-day vulnerabilities in Accellion's File Transfer Appliance (FTA) discovered in early 2021[126]. Accellion FTA was used by many Fortune 100 companies for secure file transfers, providing an attractive target for the organized crime group. The hackers exploited these vulnerabilities, leading to large-scale data breaches affecting organizations globally.

Clop's activities escalated in February 2023 when they claimed a significant intrusion success of over 130 organizations using a zero-day exploit in the GoAnywhere MFT (Managed File Transfer) software[127]. This wave of attacks was a testament to their adaptability and their ability to exploit a broad range of software vulnerabilities.

A few months later, in May 2023, the group turned their focus to the MOVEit transfer system, yet another file transfer tool frequently used by organizations. They successfully exploited the vulnerability CVE-2023-34362, allowing them to penetrate yet another file transfer and storage platform, causing severe disruption and compromise of sensitive data [128] (Table 2).

---

[126] Threatpost. (2021, February 8). Accellion FTA Zero-Day Attacks Show Ties to Clop Ransomware, FIN11. https://threatpost.com/accellion-zero-day-attacks-clop-ransomware-fin11/164150

[127] Gatlan, S. (2023, June 13). Clop ransomware claims it breached 130 orgs using GoAnywhere zero-day. BleepingComputer. www.bleepingcomputer.com/news/security/clop-ransomware-claims-it-breached-130-orgs-using-goanywhere-zero-day

[128] Downie, S., Ackerman, D., Iacono, L., & Cox, D. (2023, June 7). Clop Ransomware Exploits MOVEit Transfer Vulnerability (CVE-2023-34362). Kroll. www.kroll.com/en/insights/publications/cyber/clop-ransomware-moveit-transfer-vulnerability-cve-2023-34362

Table 2 – Clop Attacks Focused on File Transfer Software

	Accellion FTA	GoAnywhere	MOVEit
Attack Date	December 25, 2020	January 18, 2023	May 27-29, 2023
Victims Posted	January – March 2021	March 6-24, 2023	June 14, 2023 (started)
Rest Period	No new victims posted until April 13, 2023	No new victims posted until April 21, 2023	Ongoing at the time of this writing

An article published March 2023, suggested that Clop and similar cybercrime-focused groups based in Russia with Russian speaking members were tacitly supported by the Kremlin[129] and elements of the Russian government, to include the Russian Federal Security Service [130 & 131]. It is an interesting suggestion by the article's author and, if true, reinforces the concept of this chapter – *The Trickle Down Effect*.

---

[129] Gowing, B. (2023, March 8). Russian tech-hacking gang Clop: How to minimise risks. iNews. https://inews.co.uk/news/crime/russian-tech-hacking-gang-clop-minimise-risks-2397529

[130] The FSB, or Federal Security Service of the Russian Federation, is Russia's principal security agency, directly succeeding the USSR's KGB. The FSB's roles include counterintelligence, internal and border security, counterterrorism, and surveillance. While its main goal is to protect Russia's security, it also has been implicated in various activities extending beyond its borders.

131 U.S. Cybersecurity & Infrastructure Security Agency (CISA). (2022, May 9). Russian State-Sponsored and Criminal Cyber Threats to Critical Infrastructure. www.cisa.gov/news-events/cybersecurity-advisories/aa22-110a

CHAPTER 7 - THE CASTLE DOCTRINE

If you have ever been able to sit in on one of my keynotes or conference talks over the years on *"Threats, Trends, and Tactics,"* you have likely heard me walking the audience through the analogy of the castle when exploring the modern enterprise network, specifically what I have dubbed *"The Castle Doctrine"*.

I think I am fond of the analogy because audiences understand it. In movies, books, and modern retellings of historical battles, castles are the formidable strongholds designed to protect their inhabitants from external threats. Similarly, I like to draw the comparison that the modern computer network is the equivalent of a towering fortress that safeguards sensitive data and critical operations from cyberattacks, network intruders, and those seeking to abuse access.

In researching topics and chapters for this book, I studied a number of historical sources and even pulled a few books from my personal library covering ancient defensive strategies and layers of castle defense to include world history on military strategy. From fields to rock cliffs, to bounding rings of moats to narrow pathways, bridges and gates — each aspect of castle design paints a picture that we can relate to network security.

Before we get into covering castles though, I would be remiss if we did not spend a brief moment on a quote from George Patton.

> *"Fixed fortifications are monuments to the stupidity of man."*
>
> George Patton, General of the US Seventh Army

What this quote is referring to was Patton's observation of the expenditure, time, and focus of the French military on the *"The Maginot Line,"* a series of preventative and defensive fortifications built by France in the 1930s for World War 2. Ultimately, they served as a stark failure and demonstration of the perils of failing to **prepare** and **adapt** to evolving innovations, engineering advancements and strategies. Despite its impressive and costly construction as originally proposed and led by Marshal Joseph Joffre, the line was rendered ineffective when the Germans simply circumvented it (drove around it and flew over it), leading to a swift and devastating invasion of France. This scenario serves as a mirror for the challenges faced in the realm of cybersecurity, where a static defense will be easily bypassed by agile and innovative threat actors.

In contrast, George S. Patton, a renowned US military leader and strategist, recognized early on the potential of tank warfare to revolutionize land combat and the futility of static defenses that would not be able to adapt to an evolving threat which was the German Blitzkrieg strategy. His foresight and adaptability underscored the importance of anticipating and embracing change, a lesson that is equally applicable to what I execute on every week advising clients on proactive strategies, defensive network adjustments, and

Incident Response. Just as Patton understood that mechanized infantry, planes, long range artillery, and tanks would make traditional fortifications obsolete, so too must practitioners like myself in the DFIR realm continue to educate our clients, our partners, and the new generation of students entering into our industry, that evolving digital threats require dynamic and proactive defense and investigative strategies.

The failure of European military planners to foresee the impact of the German Blitzkrieg resulted in widespread devastation during World War II and success for the German army in many of its conflicts. Similarly, in the modern digital realm, the inability to anticipate and adapt to ever-changing tactics of organized criminal groups, advanced persistent groups, and lone wolves can lead to significant damage. This highlights the futility of relying solely on singular and aging cybersecurity measures and emphasizes the need for continuous innovation and adaptation in response to emerging threats.

Let us dive into another analogy. One of my favorite castles that I often interweave into my keynote talks is Caerphilly Castle, located in the town of Caerphilly[132] in South Wales. Not only is it an impressive example of medieval military architecture, but it also provides listeners with clear visual cues they can directly connect to the concepts and strategies I am discussing: For example, the leaning tower in the bottom left of the inner castle is akin to the ten-year-old server hardware propping up the growing business; the modern, aluminum-roofed building in the middle of the castle is like the fresh investment in a piece of modern computing, surrounded by walls and moats that represent InfoSec's defense-in-depth strategy; and ultimately, the

---

[132] Pronounced as *"care-philly."*

primary route into the castle in the center of the picture is like the Firewall or VPN connections in and out of the network or "*castle.*"

By way of background, Caerphilly Castle was constructed between 1268 and 1290 by Gilbert de Clare, a powerful Anglo-Norman lord, as a response to a territorial dispute with the native Welsh prince, Llywelyn ap Gruffydd. The castle was designed to demonstrate de Clare's might and to deter further Welsh incursions into his lands.[133]

The castle spans an area of approximately 30 acres, making it the largest castle in Wales and the second largest in Britain after Windsor Castle. Its design was heavily influenced by contemporary continental architecture, particularly the castles of the French region of Gascony, where de Clare had interests. Caerphilly Castle features a concentric design, comprising multiple layers of defense. The outer defenses consist of artificial lakes and moats that encircle the castle, providing a formidable barrier against potential attackers. These

---

[133] Wikipedia contributors. (2023, June 21). Caerphilly Castle. In Wikipedia, The Free Encyclopedia. https://en.wikipedia.org/wiki/Caerphilly_Castle

water features were engineered by diverting the nearby Rhymney River, which also supplied water to the castle.

The castle's outer walls are punctuated by several towers, including the prominent gatehouses, which offered additional protection and controlled access to the castle grounds. The use of twin gatehouses was a novel feature in British castle design at the time. Each gatehouse contained a portcullis and heavy doors, ensuring the security of the castle's entrances. Within the outer walls lies the inner ward, featuring a strong curtain wall and multiple defensive towers. The Great Hall, the heart of the castle's residential quarters, is located in the inner ward. These quarters provided living spaces for the lord and his retinue[134], as well as storage rooms and service areas. The castle's walls were designed to be remarkably thick, offering increased protection against siege weapons common for the day, such as trebuchets and catapults.

Caerphilly Castle's innovative design and formidable defenses played a significant role in the history of Welsh and English conflicts. The castle remained in use until the 16th century, after which it gradually fell into disrepair. Restoration efforts in the 19th and 20th centuries have since preserved parts of the castle, allowing it to stand as a testament to medieval engineering and serving as a popular tourist attraction and future bucket list item of mine. Now that we have the history lesson and the visuals, let us make the comparisons for the analogy.

---

[134] I chuckled when I read this word in one of my reference cards that I put together when collecting notes for this book. I read it maybe three times and thought I had made a typo. I had to look the word up before I remembered its meaning and in order to save you time, retinue means a group of *"advisers, assistants, or others accompanying an important person."*

DEFENSE IN DEPTH: FROM MOATS TO FIREWALLS

Caerphilly Castle was constructed with a concentric design, featuring multiple layers of defense, including moats, drawbridges, and battlements. The outer moats encircled the castle, providing a formidable barrier against intruders. The castle's drawbridges and twin gatehouses added another layer of defense, allowing defenders to control entry and exit points. In addition, the castle's walls were designed to be unusually thick, offering increased protection against siege weapons.

Similarly, defense in depth is a critical component of modern enterprise network security. It entails the implementation of multiple security controls across various layers to protect an organization's assets. These layers can include perimeter (edge) defenses such as firewalls, intrusion detection systems (IDS), intrusion prevention systems (IPS), and virtual private network (VPN) appliances, each of which serve as the modern equivalents of moats, bridges, and drawbridges — funneling and directing traffic through specific openings in the perimeter for inspection and traffic routing.

SEGMENTATION AND ACCESS CONTROL: FROM PORTCULLISES TO VLANS

Caerphilly Castle's original architects designed and included portcullises and strong gates to control access to specific areas within the fortress. Each gatehouse featured a portcullis, a heavy, vertically sliding metal or wooden grille, which could be lowered to block entry. This effectively created segmented zones that could be defended separately, even if attackers breached the outer defenses.

In a modern enterprise network, access control and segmentation are crucial. Network administrators use virtual local area networks (VLANs), access control lists (ACLs), and conditional access policies to manage access to specific network segments, zones, or portions of environments. This segmentation not only works to prevent unauthorized access, but it can also aid in stymieing actors from moving laterally and reaching additional accounts, minimizing the impact of account compromise and vulnerability exploitation.

MONITORING AND ALERTING: FROM WATCHTOWERS TO SIEM SYSTEMS

Caerphilly Castle was equipped with watchtowers and arrow loops, which provided visibility and early warning of potential threats. The castle's towers were positioned strategically to offer optimal vantage points, while the arrow loops allowed archers to fire upon attackers while remaining protected. While I'm not advocating that private sector organizations fire "*arrows*" back at attackers, there have been some CISOs, CEOs, and business owners over the years that have asked me if I knew where a particular threat actor might be physically located within the vastness of the world so they could "*just say 'hi.'*" I still remember the infosecurity team who asked if they could leverage the username, password, and IP address to login into the threat actor's jump box that had been discovered during the forensics. I advocated for sharing and leaving it to law enforcement, but you could see the wheels spinning in the team's minds.[135]

Modern enterprise networks employ similar strategies for monitoring and alerting. Security information and event management (SIEM) systems collect and analyze log data from various sources within the network, providing real-time visibility and alerting on potential threats. Network administrators can then take appropriate action to mitigate these threats before they cause damage. In addition, threat intelligence tooling, teams, and platforms allow for aggregated data collected from vastly different views and positions across the globe. As an example, and at the time of this writing, my global Incident

---

[135] "*Let me be clear…*" – I have absolutely thought about leveraging threat actor credentials to log into their infrastructure, gather intel, delete stolen data, conduct counter-recon, and all sorts of activities that accompany the litany of ideas from "*having access*," but we must remember that as much as it's wrong for criminals to trespass, it's equally not lawful to trespass the other way. Smarter people than me and attorneys can debate the ethics, legalities, and morals of "*hacking back*," but some things, in my humble opinion, are best left to federal agencies, military campaigns, and law enforcement.

Response teams at Kroll possessed experience and insights into nearly 3,200 average investigations annually, including our managed detection and response (MDR) Kroll Responder solution monitoring several hundreds of thousands of endpoints around the globe across numerous countries and regions. This near-real-time monitoring data allowed for an immense amount of telemetry to distill and hone detections for when new threat campaigns were beginning.

DEFENDING THE ENDPOINT: ARMORED GUARDS TO EDR SOLUTIONS

Caerphilly Castle relied on well-trained and armored guards to protect its inner sanctum. These guards were equipped with the latest armor and weaponry of the time, ensuring they were prepared to face any potential threats. While I think it would be epically awesome if I showed up at a client onsite and the head of information security (infosec) or Incident Response greeted me in a full suit of armor, today's analogy is a little less literal.

Computers and mobile devices can be vulnerable to malware, phishing attacks, and other threats. To counter these risks, organizations deployed antivirus solutions in the 2000s, and by now, should be evolving and transitioning fully over to managed detection and response (MDR) solutions to ensure the protection of their endpoints and, by extension, their network. In today's realm of cybersecurity, next-generation antivirus software (NGAV) and EDR sensors on endpoints connected to a network serve as the modern-day equivalent of these guards and punctuated more by the real humans that monitor and conduct "*eyes-on*" review of alerts, events, and incident data to sift through the noise and identify real threats.

In closing this chapter, I strive to always balance moments of humor in my talks, even with analogies, and what better way than to point out that at Caerphilly Castle is a wooden statue of a man holding "*up*" one of the crumbling [136] towers, akin to the 10-year-old server running in the corner of the server closet of some organizations that no one is allowed to touch because it "*just works*" or because it is running the database for the entire company.

Humorous, but more common than one might want to believe.

---

[136] https://personal.thombedford.com/wp-content/uploads/2015/05/IMG_1042.jpg

CHAPTER 8 - INCIDENT RESPONSE PLANNING & TABLETOP EXERCISES

Effective Incident Response Planning (IRP) is essential for corporations to mitigate the damage caused by cyberattacks. Cyber Incident Response planning services can help organizations develop and mature their process and procedures, identify vulnerabilities and threats, and simulate attacks to test their response capabilities. Let us explore the different types of cyber IRP services available to businesses and how they can help to protect against cyber threats.

RISK ASSESSMENT AND ANALYSIS

Risk assessment and analysis services are designed to identify potential threats and vulnerabilities to an organization's systems and data. These services typically involve reviewing an organization's existing security measures and procedures and identifying areas for improvement. I work regularly with Greg Michaels, who has been with Kroll Cyber for nearly a decade. He told me during one of our conversations that "*An effective security risk assessment process and offensive security testing can help an organization identify strengths and weaknesses in their security posture. This can help to improve their overall security program and minimize the risk of a successful cyberattack. In addition, conducting comprehensive simulated attacks, which include social engineering, can help to enhance detection and mitigation strategies for when the real day happens.*" Greg serves as a Managing Director and Global Service Line leader of Kroll's Strategy and Risk Consulting, handling proactive engagements for Kroll clients globally.

INCIDENT RESPONSE PLAN DEVELOPMENT

Incident response plan (IRP) development services help organizations develop and implement comprehensive IRPs that are tailored to their specific needs and requirements. These services typically involve assessing an organization's existing security measures and procedures, identifying potential threats and vulnerabilities, and developing a detailed plan of action in the event of a cyberattack. Erik Moser is a Managing Director within my Global DFIR Service Line and focuses on delivering expertise through Crisis Communications and Reputation Management. *"An effective Incident Response plan can help organizations minimize the impact of a security event, of an intrusion, and related data breach and help ensure the minimization of business interruption,"* said Erik. *"By developing a comprehensive Incident Response plan that is tailored to an organization's intricacies, personnel, industry vertical, supply chain vulnerabilities, and existing systems — organizations can be better prepared to respond to cyberattacks when they occur because they have modeled how they would realistically be able to respond and escalate through documentation and planning."*

INCIDENT RESPONSE PLAN REVIEW AND ENHANCEMENT

However, IRP development should not be a *"one and done"* exercise. Just as various aspects of organizations are continually changing, so too are cyberattacks and their methods. IRP review and enhancement services are designed to examine an organization's existing IRP, identify opportunities to improve, and as necessary, realign resources and priorities. These services typically involve assessing an organization's existing security measures and procedures, reviewing the Incident Response plan, and providing recommendations for enhancements.

I sat down with one of my Associate Managing Directors to discuss the service offerings and related benefits. *"By reviewing and enhancing their Incident Response plans on a regular basis, organizations can help ensure that they are prepared to identify and respond to the latest cyber threats,"* said Lucie Hayward. Cyber IRP services can help corporations develop effective plans and procedures, identify potential threats and vulnerabilities, and test their response capabilities. By investing in these services, organizations can be better prepared to respond to cyberattacks and minimize their impact on their business operations and reputation.

TABLETOP EXERCISES AND SIMULATIONS

Tabletop exercises (TTX) and related simulations are designed to test an organization's internal and external communication capabilities and responsive technology stacks in order to identify data and human detection controls as well as areas for continued improvement. These services typically involve creating a simulated cyberattack scenario and having a practitioner experienced in the investigation and remediation of the scenario's facts walk participants through how they would respond.

"Tabletop exercises and simulations help organizations identify gaps in their Incident Response plan and related processes. Ultimately, the goal is to develop more effective response strategies," said Lucie. *"In the early days, we mainly had security or IT teams participating in the exercises. But today, organizations increasingly realize that it's all hands on deck when an incident occurs. More and more, we see representatives from across the business joining the technical teams — Communications, Legal, Operations, Human Resources, etc. — which not only provides valuable perspective on previously unconsidered issues, but also helps all these team members become familiar with their roles and responsibilities. We are also running exercises for executives and board members, giving them the opportunity to consider the decisions, as well as financial and reputational implications, they might need to manage in a data security incident."*

Over the years of creating and delivering TTXs, especially for repeat clients, invigorates me to identify and build something new. Our team has identified that there are a couple of different approaches to ensuring that content remains fresh and relevant, year after year. We will schedule conversations and walk-through questions and concepts covering such items as what they would like to test or if they have experienced any incidents since the last TTX. Sometimes we find that our clients will want to build a scenario around something they experienced, either an actual incident, or an event they were able to successfully manage (from a *"what if this went south"* perspective). They may also ask us to build a scenario around something current – for example after a major vulnerability is announced we have had clients request to build in a third-party vulnerability that mimics the same phenomenon and walk them through with injects into how their team would respond.

The most important part of this experience is the client journey and making it a collaborative one. Our team provides our recommendations as the experts dealing with incidents hands on every week of every month, but after working with repeat clients, especially those that we have been through hell and back during actual incidents, the TTX experiences become ever increasingly customized and meaningful.

A list of interesting TTX topics that I have designed and presented on over the years include such ideas as the following and beyond:

- 3rd Party **Vendor Compromise** – *"What of Your Data is at Risk?"*
- **Social Media** Account Take Over – *"What Do You Do?"*
- **Insider Threats** & Intellectual Property Theft – *"Now What?"*
- Compromise Assessment – *"Cyber Nightmare Stories of **Mergers & Acquisitions (M&A)** and **Due Diligence** work."*
- **Inventory Management** – *"Its 10pm, Do You Know Where All Your Assets Are?"*
- **Data Exfil** w/out Encryption Event – *"Do You Know What They Took?"*
- Head in the Clouds – *"It's **Not Covered by EDR**, Can You Still Investigate and Protect It?"*

CHAPTER 9 - CRIMINAL GROUPS & THEIR METHODS

Organized cybercrime groups are networks of individuals who use technology to perpetrate crimes. These groups often work together in a hierarchical structure, with different members responsible for different tasks. There are several types of organized cybercrime groups, each with their own specialties and modus operandi.

FINANCIALLY MOTIVATED GROUPS

Financially motivated groups operate with the primary objective of generating profit through various cybercrime activities, using technology to steal money or financial information from individuals or organizations. These groups can range from small, independent actors to large, organized criminal syndicates with global reach. One prominent example of a financially motivated hacking group is FIN7, also known as Carbanak.[137] This group is believed to have originated in Eastern Europe and has been responsible for a range of high-profile attacks targeting financial institutions and hospitality organizations. According to the U.S. Department of Justice, by 2018, FIN7 had compromised more than 100 U.S. companies, stealing more than 15 million credit card records and causing over $1 billion in losses[138]. Despite arrests over the years and a period of inactivity, FIN7 was still going strong in 2023, as it was linked to several high-profile ransomware and other malware-related attacks.[139]

Another example of a financially motivated hacking group is Lazarus, believed to be backed by the North Korean government. Lazarus has been responsible for a range of attacks targeting financial institutions, including the 2016 cyber heist of the Bangladesh Bank, in which the group stole $81 million by exploiting vulnerabilities in the bank's computer systems.

Financially motivated hacking groups use a range of techniques to achieve their objectives, including social engineering, malware-based attacks, and

---

[137] U.S. Department of Justice. (2018, August 1). Three Members of Notorious International Cybercrime Group "Fin7" Arrested for Role in Attacking Over 100 U.S. Companies. www.justice.gov/opa/pr/three-members-notorious-international-cybercrime-group-fin7-arrested-role-attacking-over
[138] Ibid.
[139] 'Microsoft: Notorious FIN7 hackers return in Clop ransomware attacks", BleepingComputer, Sergiu Gatlan, May 19, 2023, www.bleepingcomputer.com/news/security/microsoft-notorious-fin7-hackers-return-in-clop-ransomware-attacks

ransomware attacks. These groups often operate in a highly organized and sophisticated manner, using advanced techniques to evade detection and cover their tracks.

To combat financially motivated hacking groups, law enforcement agencies and cybersecurity professionals need to have a deep understanding of threat actor tactics, techniques, and procedures (TTPs). This requires hands-on, regular experience investigating and respond to their threats, ongoing monitoring of reputable and useful threat intelligence sources and the ability to analyze and monitor across industry verticals and large enterprises to detect patterns and identify potential threats. As stated by the FBI in their 2020 Internet Crime Report, "*analyzing and disseminating threat intelligence is a critical tool for identifying and mitigating emerging cyber threats*"[140] which is exactly what Kroll's Cyber Threat Intelligence (CTI) team does every day.

---

[140] FBI. (2020). Internet Crime Report 2020. www.fbi.gov/news/stories/2019-internet-crime-report-released-021120

STATE-SPONSORED GROUPS

State-sponsored hacking groups, also known as advanced persistent threat (APT) groups, are cyber espionage units backed by nation-states or government entities. State-sponsored hacking groups are a significant threat to the national security of governments and sovereign countries as well as the stabilization of the global economy and currencies[141].

These groups operate with the primary objective of stealing sensitive information, disrupting critical infrastructure in other countries, and satisfying intelligence collection requirements of their own countries' military and intelligence silos. The techniques used by these groups are typically highly sophisticated and well-funded, often targeting high-profile targets such as government agencies, military organizations, and large multinational corporations that conduct research and development. APT groups usually operate in a covert manner with a higher likelihood of remaining undetected for extended periods of time while using greater than average techniques to evade detection.[142]

If you spend time reviewing annually released Incident Response industry reports[143], Incident Response company blogs[144], the APT Groups and Operations Google Sheet[145], and top cybersecurity news articles, you will find

---

[141] More in-depth coverage on this in Chapter 6, but think if just one criminal threat actor group can successfully move tens of millions of one country's currency (United States, Great Britain, Canada, Australia, etc.) through ransomware payments or fraudulent wire transfers through cryptocurrency (Bitcoin or Monero) conversion and then convert into the currency of the threat actor's host country, then their financial status within that country is catapulted forward and the surrounding economy of where they live, work, operate also benefits from their increased spending power.
[142] European Union Agency for Law Enforcement Cooperation (Europol). (2019). Internet Organised Crime Threat Assessment (IOCTA) 2019.
[143] www.aboutdfir.com/reading/annual-industry-reports
[144] www.kroll.com/en/insights/publications/cyber
[145] docs.google.com/spreadsheets/d/1H9_xaxQHpWaa4O_Son4Gx0YOIzleBWMsdvePFX68EKU

nearly an endless writeup of interesting and notorious state-sponsored hacking groups. Several examples are included below, but pay attention to the main themes (e.g., targets of their attacks, end goals of the attacks, and tactics involved in perpetuating their attacks):

- **APT5** (also known as **Bronze Fleetwood** or **MANGANESE**) is assessed as being a Chinese-based threat actor, active since at least 2007. They are known for targeting regional telecommunication providers and their employees in addition to high-tech manufacturing sectors and military research and defense industry sectors across United States, Europe, and Asia. APT5's attack vectors include spear-phishing, watering holes, and zero-day exploits. In 2019, reports surfaced that APT5 was aggressively exploiting vulnerabilities in Fortinet and Pulse Secure virtual private network (VPN) servers, primarily to steal information that would enable them to control the devices [146] which followed years of investigation into APT5 and its 2012 and 2015 attacks on Juniper Networks to alter source code for NetScreen firewall devices.[147]
- **APT9** (also known as **Nightshade Panda** or **FlowerLady)** is assessed as being a Chinese-associated threat actor, active since at least 2011. They are known for targeting aerospace, agriculture, energy, healthcare, media, transportation, agriculture-aligned organizations across the United States, Europe, Hong Kong, India, and South Korea to acquire data associated with proprietary information and intellectual property. APT9's attack vectors include

---

[146] "A Chinese APT is now going after Pulse Secure and Fortinet VPN servers", Catalin Cimpanu, ZDNet, Sept. 5, 2019, www.zdnet.com/article/a-chinese-apt-is-now-going-after-pulse-secure-and-fortinet-vpn-servers

[147] Bloomberg News. (2021, September 2). Juniper mystery attacks traced to Pentagon role and Chinese hackers. Bloomberg. www.bloomberg.com/news/features/2021-09-02/juniper-mystery-attacks-traced-to-pentagon-role-and-chinese-hackers

spear-phishing, valid accounts, remote services, watering holes, and custom malware. In 2015, APT9 was said to have compromised official Myanmar government websites in watering-hole attacks, infecting visitors seeking election information with a remote access trojan.

- **APT10** (also known as **Stone Panda** or **Cloud Hopper**) is assessed in open- and closed-source intelligence as being backed by the Chinese government and has been responsible for a range of cyber espionage operations targeting countries such as the United States, Japan, and the United Kingdom.[148] APT10 is known for using a range of advanced techniques, including spear-phishing attacks, watering-hole attacks, and malware-based attacks, to gain access to their target's systems.

- **APT17** (also known as **Hidden Lynx, Tailgater Team,** or **DeputyDog**) is assessed as being associated with a hacker-for-hire Chinese-based threat actor group, active since at least 2013. They are known for targeting government, military, pharmaceutical and technology organizations in the United States and Europe. APT17's attack vectors include spear-phishing, watering-hole attacks holes[149], and custom malware. This is a sophisticated, well-organized, and resourceful group that has been able to hack into major tech organizations including Adobe, Bit9, Google, Lockheed Martin, and

---

[148] "Two Chinese Hackers Associated With the Ministry of State Security Charged with Global Computer Intrusion Campaigns Targeting Intellectual Property and Confidential Business Information," U.S. Department of Justice, December 20, 2018, www.justice.gov/opa/pr/two-chinese-hackers-associated-ministry-state-security-charged-global-computer-intrusion. Also, "US and UK accuse China of sustained hacking campaign," The Guardian, Patrick Wintour, December 20, 2018, www.theguardian.com/world/2018/dec/20/us-and-uk-accuse-china-of-sustained-hacking-campaign

[149] Symantec Corporation. (2023). Internet Security Threat Report (ISTR) 15 April, Volume 20. https://docs.broadcom.com/doc/istr-15-april-volume-20-en

RSA. They have been known to target hundreds of companies at the same time across geographic locations. As an example of their resourcefulness, when they were unable get past controls at U.S. defense contractors, that used the Bit9 trust-based software, they turned their sights on Bit9 itself. APT9 was ultimately able to compromise the Bit9 network[150], identify how files were being digitally signed during the code creation process, and ultimately inserted a number of their own malicious files into the Bit9 development to production processes which were ultimately then pushed down to Bit9 customers allowing for APT9 to access the targets they wanted in the first place.[151]

- **APT18** (also known as **Wekby** or **Dynamite Panda** or **TA428**) is assessed as being associated with a Chinese-based threat actor, active since at least 2009. They are known for targeting defense, construction, technology, financial services, human rights, and healthcare organizations in the United States and Europe. APT18's attack vectors include spear-phishing, watering holes, and custom malware. In 2014, an attack on Community Health Systems that compromised the personal information of 4.5 million patients, was attributed to APT18.[152]

---

[150] Schwartz, M. J. (2013). Chinese "Hidden Lynx" Hackers Launch Widespread APT Attacks. Dark Reading. www.darkreading.com/attacks-breaches/chinese-hidden-lynx-hackers-launch-widespread-apt-attacks

[151] "Hidden Lynx – Professional Hackers for Hire", A.L. Johnson, Symantec/Broadcom, September 17, 2013, https://community.broadcom.com/symantecenterprise/communities/community-home/librarydocuments/viewdocument?DocumentKey=8962de07-8e6a-41cc-a6d6-d22ea52dcbfa&CommunityKey=1ecf5f55-9545-44d6-b0f4-4e4a7f5f5e68&tab=librarydocuments

[152] "APT Gang Branches Out to Medical Espionage in Community Health Breach", Michael Mimoso, Threatpost, August 19, 2014, https://threatpost.com/apt-gang-branches-out-to-medical-espionage-in-community-health-breach/107828

- **APT19** (also known as **Deep Panda** or **Shell Crew** or **KungFu Kittens**) is most often assessed as a group of freelancers with a nexus to the Chinese government. Their attack vectors include spear-phishing, watering holes, zero-day vulnerabilities, and custom malware. They are known to target organizations in a wide variety of industries and gained notoriety in 2014 with attacks on the U.S. Office of Personnel Management (OPM), major health insurer Anthem, two firms that conducted federal background checks, and Australian media organizations ahead of that year's G20 Summit, among others.[153] More recently, in 2022, the group reportedly capitalized on the Log4Shell vulnerability[154] *"to spread a new, 'novel' rootkit"*[155] on victim systems.

- **APT27** (also known **Bronze Union, Emissary Panda, Iron Tiger,** or **G0027**) is a threat actor assessed as being based in China. They have been active since at least 2009 and have targeted government and contractors, gaming, gambling, and technology organizations in the United States, Europe, and Asia. They are a highly resourceful and agile group that employs numerous attack vectors, to include *"watering holes, spear phishing, remote code execution, living off the land attack,*

---

[153] "APT group: APT 19, Deep Panda, C0d0so0", Electronic Transactions Development Agency. https://apt.etda.or.th/cgi-bin/showcard.cgi?g=APT%2019%2C%20Deep%20Panda%2C%20C0d0so0&n=1

[154] In December 2021, reports surfaced about a vulnerability that affected the Apache Log4j Java logging library, which is widely used in many client and server applications. The Log4j utility is commonly included in Java-based third-party enterprise software and multiple Apache frameworks. If exploited, the vulnerability could facilitate remote code execution or exfiltrate sensitive environmental variables. The vulnerability, labeled as 10 *"critical"*, was commonly referred to as Log4j or Log4Shell and was assigned a Common Vulnerabilities and Exposures ("CVE") number of CVE-2021-44228.

[155] "Chinese hackers Deep Panda return with Log4Shell exploits, new Fire Chili rootkit", Charlie Osborne, ZDNet, April 1, 2022, www.zdnet.com/article/chinese-hackers-deep-panda-return-with-log4shell-exploits-new-fire-chili-rootkit

rootkit attack, supply chain attack, [and] unauthorized access"[156]. In 2023, APT27 has reportedly turned its focus on compromising organizations running devices on the Linux operating system.[157] One of the interesting aspects of APT27 targeting gaming and gambling sites is the age-old counterintelligence aspect of identifying individuals that have gambling debt so as to offer then a lifeline and then recruit them for intelligence gathering and spy operations in the real world. This is a world that I used to be a part of when I was a Special Agent for the FBI. Identifying sources of information through Human Intelligence (HUMINT) operations.

- **APT28** (also known as **FANCY BEAR** or **Strontium**) is assessed as being a Russian-based threat actor, active since at least 2014. They are known for targeting government, military, and media organizations in the United States and Europe. APT28's attack vectors include spear-phishing, watering holes, and zero-day exploits. For example, APT28 used spear-phishing emails to deliver malware that allowed the attackers to steal sensitive data from the 2016 Democratic National Committee. In June 2023, APT28 reportedly compromised Ukraine email servers, including ones used by Ukraine government agencies[158]. A few months earlier, in April 2023, the U.S. National Security Agency, U.S. Cybersecurity and Infrastructure Security Agency, FBI, and the U.K. National Cyber

---

[156] "APT27: An In-depth Analysis of a Decade-Old Active Chinese Threat Group", Cyware Blog. www.cyware.com/resources/research-and-analysis/apt27-an-in-depth-analysis-of-a-decade-old-active-chinese-threat-group-e4cc, March 29, 2022.
[157] "Chinese state-backed hackers Iron Tiger target Linux devices with new malware", Claudia Glover, Tech Monitor, March 2, 2023, https://techmonitor.ai/technology/cybersecurity/apt27-iron-tiger-chinese-hackers-linux
[158] "Russian APT28 hackers breach Ukrainian govt email servers," Sergiu Gatlan, BleepingComputer.com, June 20, 2023, www.bleepingcomputer.com/news/security/russian-apt28-hackers-breach-ukrainian-govt-email-servers/

Security Centre released a joint advisory on methods used by APT28 to exploit and gain access to Cisco routers.[159]

- **APT29** (also known as **COZY BEAR**) is assessed in open- and closed-source intelligence as being backed by the Russian government and has been responsible for a range of high-profile attacks, including (alongside APT28 Fancy Bear) the 2016 hack of the Democratic National Committee in the United States. APT29 is known for using advanced malware and social engineering techniques to infiltrate target networks and steal sensitive information.

- **APT31** (also known as **Zirconium**) is a threat actor assessed as being affiliated with the Chinese government. APT31's attack vectors include spear-phishing, watering holes, and custom malware. Researchers have observed APT31 targeting third parties such as law firms and managed services providers (MSPs) in order to get to their clients, APT31's true targets. In 2021, France issued an advisory that APT31 was using a *"network of compromised home routers as operational relay boxes in order to perform stealth reconnaissance as well as attacks"* on French organizations[160], and in 2022, researchers discovered APT31 attacks against Russian enterprises[161].

- **APT33** (also known as **GAUSS** or **OilRig**) is a threat actor assessed as being affiliated with the North Korean government. They have

---

[159] "APT28 exploits known vulnerability to carry out reconnaissance and deploy malware on Cisco routers, April 2023, https://media.defense.gov/2023/Apr/18/2003202295/-1/-1/0/CSA_APT28_EXPLOITS_KNOWN_VULNERABILITY.PDF

[160] "France warns of APT31 cyberspies targeting French organizations", Sergiu Gatlan, BleepingComputer.com, July 21, 2021, www.bleepingcomputer.com/news/security/france-warns-of-apt31-cyberspies-targeting-french-organizations

[161] "APT31 group attacks Russian energy and media companies," Positive Technologies, August 4, 2022, www.ptsecurity.com/ww-en/about/news/apt31-group-attacks-russian-energy-and-media-companies

been active since at least 2014 and have targeted financial institutions, energy companies, and government organizations in Asia and Europe. APT 33's attack vectors include spear-phishing, watering holes, and custom malware.

- **APT35** (also known as **CHARMING KITTEN or PHOSPHORUS or TA453**) has reportedly been linked to the Iranian government. APT35's attack vectors include spear-phishing, social engineering, and custom malware, with targets that typically include U.S. and Middle Eastern government personnel, as well as information technology, media, engineering, business services and telecommunications sectors. In July 2021, Meta (Facebook's parent company) shared action it took against APT35 *"to disrupt their ability to use their infrastructure to abuse our platform, distribute malware and conduct espionage operations across the internet, targeting primarily the United States."*[162] More recently, in June 2023, reports surfaced that APT35 was using spear phishing to distribute updated backdoor malware to journalists in Israel[163]

- **APT41** (also known as **WICKED PANDA, WINNTI GROUP**, or **G0096**) is a threat actor assessed as being based in China. They have been active since at least 2016 and have targeted government, military, and technology organizations in the United States, Europe, and Asia. APT41's attack vectors include spear-phishing, watering holes, and custom malware. APT41's activities have landed purported group members on an FBI Most List, after the Chinese nationals were indicted for a long laundry list of charges: "The

---

[162] "Taking Action Against Hackers in Iran", Mike Dvilyanski and David Agranovich, Meta, July 15, 2021, www.about.fb.com/news/2021/07/taking-action-against-hackers-in-iran/
[163] "Iran-Linked APT35 Targets Israeli Media With Upgraded Spear-Phishing Tools", Dan Raywood, Dark Reading, June 30, 2023, www.darkreading.com/dr-global/iran-linked-apt35-israeli-media-upgraded-spear-phishing

defendants allegedly conducted supply chain attacks to gain unauthorized access to networks throughout the world, targeting hundreds of companies representing a broad array of industries to include: social media, telecommunications, government, defense, education, and manufacturing. These victims included companies in Australia, Brazil, Germany, India, Japan and Sweden. The defendants allegedly targeted telecommunications providers in the United States, Australia, China (Tibet), Chile, India, Indonesia, Malaysia, Pakistan, Singapore, South Korea, Taiwan, and Thailand. The defendants allegedly deployed ransomware attacks and demanded payments from victims."[164]

- **APT52** (also known as **BlackTech** or **BRONZE UNION**) is a threat actor assessed as being based in China. They have been active since at least 2017 and have targeted government, military, and technology organizations in the United States, Europe, and Asia. APT52 is recognized for their use of custom malware and their ability to maintain access to compromised systems for long periods of time.

Government intelligence agencies leverage a range of techniques to covertly (spy) collect knowledge on neighboring and foreign governments. The ultimate goal of state-sponsored hacking groups is to provide their governments with a strategic advantages by collecting intelligence that can inform policy decisions, military strategies, or economic plans. The specific intelligence collection requirements for each group will depend on the strategic interests and geopolitical goals of their host country. No matter the

---

[164] "APT 41 GROUP – Most Wanted", Federal Bureau of Investigation, www.fbi.gov/wanted/cyber/apt-41-group

method, the goal of spying remains the same - *"being in the know"* before someone else.

As far back as 1948 in the book *"Intelligence is for Commanders"* by Military Service Publishing Company, there has been a focus on the cycle of intelligence gathering by military complexes, nation states, and covert operating groups. As the world around us has evolved over the past decades, especially in the world of technology, digitally enhanced capabilities, and cyber overall as a warfare and intelligence category of operations, the focus of intelligence-based principles has remained largely unchanged. *"The basic and elemental principle of military intelligence is embodied in the relationship between four major features: The collection of information, the processing of this information to produce intelligence, the use of the resulting intelligence, and the direction of the collection effort."*[165]

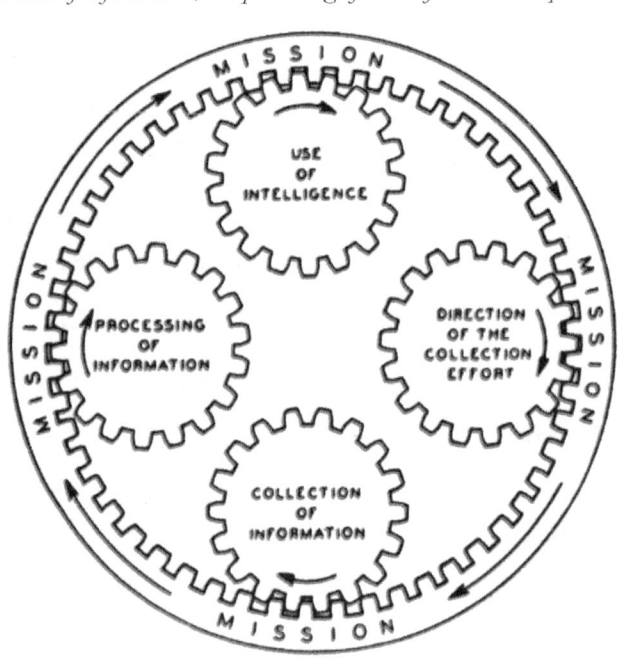

Figure 1 – *"Intelligence is for Commanders"* by By Robert Rigby Glass, Philip Buford Davidson

---

[165] Glass, R. R., Davidson, P. B. (1948). Intelligence is for Commanders. United States: Military Service Publishing Company.

HACKTIVIST GROUPS

Modern hacktivist groups use hacking and technology as a means of exciting and invoking political activism and pushing agendas that reflect their interpretation of what social justice can be. These groups often target governments, corporations, and other organizations that they believe are engaged in unethical or unjust activities. One prominent example of a modern hacktivist group is the Anonymous group, a loosely organized collective of activists who use hacking and other digital tools to protest against a range of social and political issues[166]. The group gained prominence for its various cyberattacks against governments, institutions, and corporations, advocating for freedom of speech and information transparency.

Aubrey Cottle, also known as Kirtaner, is often credited as one of the key founders of Anonymous. In an interview with Vice in 2020, Cottle explained that the group initially started as an offshoot of the imageboard 4chan[167] community: "*The stuff that we were doing on 4chan back in the day was just for the laughs. We didn't really have any sort of political motivation or anything like that.*"[168] However, the group's focus shifted over time. Anonymous' self-professed end game is to be seen by the world's audience of internet viewers as promoting their vision of transparency, fighting against perceived censorship. Anonymous has a documented history of reliance upon on DDoS (distributed denial of service) attacks, website defacement, and doxing

---

[166] "What is Anonymous? How the infamous 'hacktivist' group went from 4chan trolling to launching cyberattacks on Russia", CNBC, Tom Huddleston Jr., March 25, 2022, www.cnbc.com/2022/03/25/what-is-anonymous-the-group-went-from-4chan-to-cyberattacks-on-russia.html
[167] www.4chan.org
[168] Cottle, A. (2023, June 10). "I Left Anonymous. Now I'm Back" www.youtube.com/watch?v=sNEA0sglO5A

(releasing personal information). The collective often used social media and other online platforms to coordinate and communicate.

One of the group's earliest and most well-known hacking campaigns was "*Project Chanology*" in 2008, which targeted the Church of Scientology. Anonymous accused the church of suppressing information and launched a series of DDoS attacks, defaced websites, and organized protests. Another notable instance of Anonymous' hacking activities was the 2010 "*Operation Payback*" campaign, in which the group targeted companies like MasterCard, Visa, and PayPal for their refusal to process donations to WikiLeaks. The group used DDoS attacks to disrupt these companies' websites and services.

This is around the timeframe of heightened FBI cyber and criminal task force focus on this group. I remember one particular search warrant that I was a part of, executed in the Middle District of North Carolina by a number of FBI agents, and the exact moment that an Agent lifted the Guy Fawkes mask from behind a chair in our subject's bedroom. There is nothing quite like interviewing a subject about why they hacked, trespassed, and gained unauthorized access into a private business's servers and network and having them deny it when you know how the conversation is about to go. The look on the subject's face when the Agent pulled the mask out of an evidence box along with numerous other articles of evidence that linked them to the exact crime outlined in the FBI's criminal complaint, was — in a word — priceless.

It is important to note that Anonymous does not have a centralized leadership structure, and its members were often self-proclaimed activists — leading to decentralized thoughts, tactics, and techniques. For example, in 2022, Anonymous targeted Russian officials after that country's invasion of

Ukraine[169], but more recently, in April 2023, a group calling itself "*Anonymous Sudan*", considered to be part of the larger Anonymous collective, has sided with Russia and engaged in attacks against Ukraine.[170] Anonymous Sudan also took credit for disrupting Microsoft Outlook.com in June 2023 via DDOS attacks "*to protest the US getting involved in Sudanese internal affairs.*"[171] As a result, it was difficult in my estimation to ever pin down an overarching end game for the entire group. However, the common thread that runs through their activities is their pursuit of ostensibly a "*higher purpose*", e.g., promoting transparency, justice, or freedom of information.

Another example of a hacktivist group of note was LulzSec, short for Lulz Security, which gained notoriety as early as 2011 for their high-profile attacks, the humorous tone of their announcements, and their self-proclaimed motivation to carry out hacks for "*lulz*" or laughs — a trend born of internet sociology on internet forums, bulletin boards, and private conversation channels. [172] The group was loosely associated with the Anonymous collective, but they also maintained their own distinct identity. LulzSec employed a variety of hacking techniques, including SQL injection, DDoS attacks, and social engineering, to infiltrate their targets. They exfiltrated sensitive data such as passwords, email addresses, and internal documentation from their targets and then, foreshadowing ransomware threat actor groups to come, would publish this information on platforms

---

[169] "Anonymous: How hackers are trying to undermine Putin", BBC, March 20, 2022, www.bbc.com/news/technology-60784526
[170] "What You Need to Know About the Anonymous Sudan Hacker Group", Cyesec Ltd., April 4, 2023, https://cyesec.com/blog/what-you-need-to-know-about-the-anonymous-sudan-hacker-group
[171] "Outlook.com hit by outages as hacktivists claim DDoS attacks", BleepingComputer.com, June 6, 2023, www.bleepingcomputer.com/news/microsoft/outlookcom-hit-by-outages-as-hacktivists-claim-ddos-attacks/
[172] "LulzSec: what they did, who they were and how they were caught", The Guardian, Charles Arthur, May 16, 2013, www.theguardian.com/technology/2013/may/16/lulzsec-hacking-fbi-jail

like Pastebin or their own website. The group would often announce their exploits on their Twitter account, @LulzSec, where they amassed tens of thousands of followers. One of LulzSec's core beliefs was that they were exposing the weak security of their targets — an interesting mantra that has also carried over into many ransomware threat actor groups who attempt to justify their network intrusions, data exfiltration, and ransom demands under the guise of an *"unscheduled penetration test."* LulzSec's reign of cyberattacks was defining, but relatively short-lived, as the group largely disbanded in June 2011 after approximately 50 days of activity. Despite their brief existence, LulzSec's high-profile attacks significantly impacted public awareness of cybersecurity and prompted a renewed focus on securing digital infrastructure.

At the time of the writing of this book, the *"IT Army of Ukraine"* and a Russian-affiliated group called Killnet, were locked in disruptive attacks against, not only each other, but each other's countries and government networks and related websites. Hacktivism was at the center, globally, of these groups actively fighting a war in cyberspace, while a physical ground war played out in front of the world between the two countries. The Ukrainian government was taking outspoken, and well documented steps leveraging online social media and Telegram channels to send out international requests for volunteers to *"help fight the cyber war by joining the IT army of Ukraine."* [173]

Modern hacktivist groups use a range of techniques to achieve their objectives, including website defacement, DDoS attacks, and data theft. These groups often operate in a highly decentralized and anonymous manner,

---

[173] Layton, J. (2023). 'Cyber battlefield' map shows attacks being played out live across the globe. Metro. https://metro.co.uk/2023/07/03/cyber-battlefield-map-shows-attacks-played-out-live-across-the-globe-19058014/

using social media and other online platforms to coordinate their activities. Combating the activities of these groups requires ongoing monitoring and analysis of the threat landscape and close collaboration between law enforcement agencies and cybersecurity professionals.

SG93IG1hbnkgcHJvZ3JhbW1lcnMgZG8gcW91IG5lZWQgdG8gY2hhbmdlIGEgbGlnaH
RidWxiPyBOb25lLiBXaHkgYm90aGVyPyBUaGUgbGlnaHQgZnJvbSB0aGUgc2NyZWV
uIGlzIGVub3VnaCB0byBrZWVwIHByb2dyYW1taW5nLg==

LAUNDERING MONEY VIA CRYPTO

Cryptocurrencies have become a popular means for cybercriminals to launder money obtained from illegal activities, such as ransomware attacks. Cryptocurrencies such as Bitcoin, Ethereum, and Monero [174] offer cybercriminals a high degree of anonymity and security when it comes to laundering money. Also, unlike traditional financial transactions,

---

[174] Bitcoin, Ethereum, and Monero are all digital or virtual cryptocurrencies that use encryption techniques to secure and verify transactions and control the creation of new units. Bitcoin (BTC) is the first and most well-known cryptocurrency, which was created in 2009 by an anonymous person or group known as Satoshi Nakamoto. It operates on a decentralized peer-to-peer network and has a limited supply of 21 million coins. Bitcoin is often used as a store of value or a means of payment, and its value can be volatile. Ethereum (ETH) is another popular cryptocurrency that was launched in 2015 by Vitalik Buterin. It is a decentralized platform that allows developers to build and deploy decentralized applications (dApps) using smart contracts, which are self-executing contracts with the terms of the agreement between buyer and seller being directly written into code. Ethereum also has its own cryptocurrency called Ether, which is used to pay for transactions and computational services on the network. Monero (XMR) is a privacy-focused cryptocurrency that was launched in 2014. It uses advanced cryptographic techniques to obscure the identity of users and the details of transactions. Monero is designed to be more anonymous and untraceable than other cryptocurrencies like Bitcoin, and it is often used by people who want to keep their financial transactions private or avoid surveillance.

cryptocurrency transactions are not subject to the same regulatory oversight and are difficult to trace.

The basic process of laundering money via cryptocurrency involves converting the ill-gotten gains into cryptocurrency, transferring the cryptocurrency to multiple wallets to obscure its origin, and then converting it back into fiat currency via a cryptocurrency exchange or other means. Ransomware attacks are a common method used by cybercriminals to obtain funds that can be laundered via cryptocurrency.[175] In a typical ransomware attack, the attacker will encrypt the victim's data and demand payment in exchange for the decryption key. Over the past few years, we have seen ransomware attacks evolve as threat actors additionally exfiltrate data and threaten to publicize/sell data if the ransom is not paid. More and more, we are seeing threat actors bypassing encryption altogether and just exfiltrating data, with the same ransom demand. In all cases, the payment is requested in cryptocurrency.

Ransomware attackers use a variety of techniques to launder the cryptocurrency obtained from their attacks. One technique is to use mixing services, which shuffle the cryptocurrency among multiple wallets to obscure its origin. Another technique is to use peer-to-peer marketplaces, which allow buyers and sellers to trade cryptocurrency anonymously. Attackers may also use darknet marketplaces to cash out their illicit gains, or they may convert the cryptocurrency to fiat currency via unregulated exchanges. Tracking and preventing money laundering via cryptocurrency can be challenging tasks given the anonymity, security features of cryptocurrency transactions, and crypto exchanges globally that may not cooperate with law enforcement

---

[175] Chainalysis. (2020). Crypto Crime Report: Decoding Darknet Markets, Ponzi Schemes, and Ransomware.

processes. However, there are several techniques that can be used to monitor and detect suspicious transactions, including blockchain analysis, IP address tracking, and user profiling. Additionally, law enforcement agencies are increasing their efforts to combat money laundering via cryptocurrency, with several high-profile arrests and seizures of cryptocurrency funds in recent years.

Mitigating the risk of ransomware attacks and money laundering via cryptocurrency involves a multi-layered approach to cybersecurity. This may include implementing robust security measures to prevent or recover from ransomware attacks, such as regular software updates and backups. Additionally, organizations can educate their employees about the risks of ransomware attacks and provide training on how to avoid them. To prevent money laundering via cryptocurrency, organizations can use cryptocurrency tracking tools and implement strict Know Your Customer (KYC) and Anti-Money Laundering (AML) policies. Money laundering via cryptocurrency is an increasingly common practice among cybercriminals, with ransomware attacks serving as a major source of illicit funds. By understanding the techniques used by ransomware attackers to launder cryptocurrency, organizations can take steps to prevent these attacks and mitigate the risks associated with money laundering via cryptocurrency.[176]

---

[176] National Cyber Security Centre (NCSC). (2020). Ransomware: Guidance for Organizations.

THE DIGITAL FRONTIER – NORTH KOREA'S CRYPTO HEISTS

In the landscape of international finance, a new battlefield has emerged. This battlefield is not marked by physical weaponry, but by digital tools and cryptocurrencies. The central figure in this narrative is North Korea, a nation that has leveraged the power of the digital world to directly fund its ballistic missile program and lessen the effect of international sanctions upon its financial sector. As reported by The Wall Street Journal[177], North Korea's cyber army has allegedly stolen over $3 billion in cryptocurrencies between 2018 and 2023.

The North Korean hacker groups, notably the Lazarus Group, have been implicated in some of the most substantial crypto heists in history[178]. One such incident involved the hack of Axie Infinity's Ronin blockchain[179], where the hackers absconded with about $625 million worth of Ethereum and USDC. This event marked one of the largest crypto thefts ever recorded, and it was executed with a level of sophistication that has raised alarm bells among international observers.

The method of attack was as ingenious as it was effective. The hackers posed as a recruiter and reached out to an engineer at Sky Mavis, the gaming company behind Axie Infinity. They then implanted a trojan horse, a malicious computer code, onto the engineer's computer. This gave them access to Sky Mavis and its customers, and the private keys required for

---

[177] The Wall Street Journal. (2023). How North Korea's Hacker Army Stole $3 Billion in Crypto, Funding Nuclear Program. www.wsj.com/articles/how-north-koreas-hacker-army-stole-3-billion-in-crypto-funding-nuclear-program-d6fe8782

[178] New York Times. (2023, April 24). U.S. Indicts Four Men in Scheme to Launder Cryptocurrency for North Korea. www.nytimes.com/2023/04/24/us/politics/justice-dept-cryptocurrency-north-korea.html

[179] Zirlin, J. (2023, March 30). Axie Infinity's Ronin Blockchain Overhauls Tech, Expands to New IP on Anniversary of $625M Hack. www.coindesk.com/tech/2023/03/30/axie-infinitys-ronin-blockchain-overhauls-tech-expands-to-new-ip-on-anniversary-of-600m-hack

validating transactions. This audacious theft caught the attention of the U.S. government, which has since intensified its focus on countering such attacks. In April, the U.S. Treasury revealed that North Korean hackers and scammers exploit loopholes in the decentralized finance (DeFi) space to launder money and hide criminal activity.

The focus of North Korean cyber activities has shifted from traditional espionage or attack capabilities to generating cash. Their cybercriminals have become more technically proficient, pulling off elaborate maneuvers that have not been observed anywhere else. It is believed that thousands of IT workers, including government officials and freelance Japanese blockchain developers, are linked to the regime's cybercrime operations. North Korea's focus on cyber theft has resulted in heists like the $81,000,000 stolen from the central bank of Bangladesh in 2016. They have also made over $100,000 from a quickly spreading worm called WannaCry. However, nothing has been as profitable as their string of attacks on crypto, which began in earnest in 2018.

North Korea crypto heists continue as of this writing, with reports linking the Lazarus Group in a June 2023 incident where $100 million in cryptoassets was stolen from Atomic Wallet users.[180]

More recently at the time of this book's research and writing, hackers linked to North Korea pulled off a cascading supply chain attack. They targeted and conducted a longcon operation to compromise not just one, but two separate software manufacturers, one at a time with an end goal of inserting malicious code into their products and leveraging that maliciousness to target and

---

[180] "North Korean hackers stole $100 million in recent cryptocurrency heist, analysts say", Raphael Satter, Reuters, June 13, 2023, www.reuters.com/world/north-korean-hackers-stole-100-million-recent-cryptocurrency-heist-analysts-2023-06-13

leapfrog to another intended target. A report by Mandiant documented what they observed as a double supply chain attack methodology resulting in Trading Technologies being the first victim[181] in which a trojanized version of specific Trading Technologies' software was assessed as having been downloaded by an employee of 3CX, a software development company, which was the second targeted victim in the double supply chain attack. The North Koreans then used access to 3CX systems to trojanize that firm's software as a completion of their supply chain compromise objectives. From there, they leveraged the 3CX software attack to identify, target, and leapfrog into customer networks of 3CX, including targeting cryptocurrency exchanges.

---

[181] Mandiant. (2023, March 29). 3CX Software Supply Chain Compromise Initiated by a Prior Software Supply Chain Compromise; Suspected North Korean Actor Responsible. Mandiant Blog. www.mandiant.com/resources/blog/3cx-software-supply-chain-compromise

CUSTOM MALWARE DEVELOPMENT

Custom malware development is a technique used by cybercriminal groups and hackers to create tailored malware that is specifically designed to evade detection and bypass security controls. According to Cole Manaster, Head of Malware Analysis and Reverse Engineering at Kroll, this type of malware is not necessarily more sophisticated than off-the-shelf malware; the key is its customization for the target's network environment: *"Threat actors develop and deploy custom malware to bypass specific security controls being used by an intended victim. At the end of the day, it's often a "cost-benefit" proposition — the threat actors must have an incentive or expect a significant reward from compromising the specific target to spend the time and resources to develop custom malware. Because the malware is designed to interface seamlessly in the victim's environment, detecting it can be extremely difficult. For example, APTs, well-known for their custom malware, try to be quiet in the environment as they fulfill their objective, which often is long-term information-gathering."*

Custom malware can take a range of forms, including remote access trojans (RATs), keyloggers, and rootkits, for a variety of malicious activities, including data theft, espionage, and ransomware attacks. Cole noted that today, non-APT cybercriminals have found a lower *"barrier to entry"* via specialized malware development kits or services, which allow even novice actors to create customized malware. These kits and services can be purchased on underground marketplaces and are designed to be easy to use, requiring little technical knowledge or resources. According to a report by the cybersecurity firm Carbon Black, "*malware development kits and services have become increasingly popular among cybercriminals, as they allow criminals to create custom malware without needing to invest significant resources in research and development.*"[182]

---

[182] Carbon Black. (2018, October). Modern Malware Development: A Kit for Today's Threat Landscape. www.carbonblack.com/wp-content/uploads/2018/10/Modern-Malware-Development.pdf

To combat the use of custom malware by cybercriminal groups and hackers, law enforcement agencies and cybersecurity professionals need to have a deep understanding of the tactics, techniques, and procedures (TTPs) used by these actors. This requires ongoing monitoring of the underground cybercrime market and the analysis of threat intelligence sources to identify potential threats. As stated by the U.S. Federal Bureau of Investigation (FBI) in their 2022 Internet Crime Report, "*the FBI works closely with the private sector and other partners to identify, disrupt, and dismantle cybercriminal enterprises, including those involved in the development and deployment of custom malware.*"

POLYMORPHIC MALWARE

One of the most insidious forms of malware is polymorphic malware, which is designed to evade detection by constantly changing its code and structure. Polymorphic malware has been around since the 1990s, when the first polymorphic virus, known as the "*Chameleon*" virus, was discovered.[183] Since then, cybercriminals have been continually using obfuscation, encryption, and code generation to develop increasingly sophisticated polymorphic malware[184]. In recent years, polymorphic malware has become a favorite tool of APT groups and other highly skilled attackers due to its ability to evade detection and persist on compromised systems.

Polymorphic malware is designed to change its code and structure each time it is executed, making it difficult for traditional antivirus and malware detection solutions to identify and stop the malware. Polymorphic malware can also be designed to avoid detection by anti-malware solutions by checking for the presence of virtual machines, sandboxes, or other security measures that may be used for analysis. There have been several high-profile attacks involving polymorphic malware in recent years. One example is the Stuxnet worm, which was designed to target and disrupt Iran's nuclear program. Stuxnet used advanced polymorphic techniques to evade detection and propagate through a network of air-gapped systems.

Another example is the Emotet trojan, which was discovered in 2014 and went on to become one of the most prevalent and prolific malware threats of the years that immediately followed. Emotet used a sophisticated polymorphic engine that allowed it to evade detection and persist on infected

---

[183] Knowledge Year – 1990, Kaspersky, encyclopedia.kaspersky.com/knowledge/year-1990
[184] "BlackMamba: Using AI to Generate Polymorphic Malware", Security Boulevard, Jeff Sims, March 7, 2023, https://securityboulevard.com/2023/03/blackmamba-using-ai-to-generate-polymorphic-malware

systems. Despite the seizure of its infrastructure via a multinational law enforcement effort in 2021[185] and famous for periodically *"going on hiatus,"* Emotet attacks routinely resurged with novel features, attack vectors, and tactics. For example, after dropping from sight in late 2022, Emotet resurfaced in the early part of 2023 with new tactics that included *"instructing victims to move the decoy Microsoft Excel files to the default Office Templates folder in Windows, a location trusted by the operating system, to execute malicious macros embedded within the documents to deliver Emotet"*[186] and with an email spam campaign where the actors *"use binary padding as an evasion technique, where both the dropper document and the Emotet DLL files are inflated to 500+ megabytes to avoid security solutions."*[187]

Detecting polymorphic malware can be a challenging task due to its constantly changing code and structure. However, there are several techniques that can be used to detect and mitigate the threat of polymorphic malware.[188] One of the most effective techniques is behavior-based detection, which involves monitoring the behavior of the malware to identify suspicious activity. Another approach is signature-based detection, which involves comparing the malware code to a database of known malware signatures. However, this technique can be less effective against polymorphic malware, which may change its code and structure to avoid detection. Given the evolving nature of polymorphic malware, it is important to employ a multi-layered approach to security to mitigate the threat. This may include

---

[185] "World's most dangerous malware EMOTET disrupted through global action", Europol, January 27, 2021, www.europol.europa.eu/media-press/newsroom/news/world%E2%80%99s-most-dangerous-malware-emotet-disrupted-through-global-action

[186] "Emotet Malware Makes a Comeback with New Evasion Techniques", The Hacker News, January 24, 2023, https://thehackernews.com/2023/01/emotet-malware-makes-comeback-with-new.html

[187] "Emotet Returns, Now Adopts Binary Padding for Evasion", Trend Micro, March 13, 2023, www.trendmicro.com/en_us/research/23/c/emotet-returns-now-adopts-binary-padding-for-evasion.html

[188] Singh, R., & Mishra, A. (2020). Polymorphic Malware Analysis and Detection Techniques: A Survey. IEEE Transactions on Computational Social Systems

implementing behavior-based detection tools, using anti-malware solutions that incorporate polymorphic detection techniques, and regularly updating software and security patches to prevent vulnerabilities from being exploited. Additionally, educating users about the risks of malware and providing training on best practices for cybersecurity can help prevent malware infections and minimize the impact of successful attacks. Polymorphic malware represents a significant and continued threat to computer systems and networks. By understanding the characteristics of polymorphic malware and implementing effective detection and mitigation strategies, organizations can minimize the risk of infection and reduce the impact of successful attacks.

MALWARE AS A SERVICE (MAAS)

Malware as a Service (MaaS) is a cybercrime model that allows criminals to purchase and use custom-built malware without requiring significant technical knowledge or resources. This model is similar to Software as a Service (SaaS) and Infrastructure as a Service (IaaS), where users can purchase access to software or infrastructure without needing to own or manage their own resources.

MaaS providers offer a range of services, including custom-built malware, support, and training, to their customers. This allows even novice cybercriminals to launch sophisticated attacks against their targets. MaaS providers also offer a range of pricing models, including pay-per-use or subscription-based pricing, making it easier for criminals to manage their costs, which can be amazingly low. For example, in 2017, an infostealer offered through via MaaS was going for only $7 - $13, despite having encrypted executables and the ability to *"target multiple applications and browsers, including Google Chrome, Opera, FileZilla, Amigo, Kometa, Torch, and Orbitum..."*[189]

MaaS has been used in a range of cybercrime activities, including ransomware attacks, credential theft, and botnet deployment. The use of MaaS has also led to an increase in the number and sophistication of cyberattacks, as more criminals and novice players are able to access a broader array of tooling and resources. One of the things that I have explained to clients over the years (and noted how it routinely surprises many of them) is that organized crime groups operate as businesses — because they are. Unethical and immoral in operation and focus, sure, but the ransomware epidemic has fueled an

---

[189] "Two New Platforms Found Offering Cybercrime-as-a-Service to 'Wannabe Hackers'", The Hacker News, Swati Khandelwal, July 15, 2017, https://thehackernews.com/2017/07/cybercrime-as-as-service.html

amazing surge of junior and novice cybercriminals looking for their payday in the form of a large ransomware payment.

To combat the use of MaaS, cybersecurity professionals need to have a deep understanding of the underground cybercrime market and the tactics, techniques, and procedures (TTPs) used by MaaS providers. This requires ongoing monitoring of dark web marketplaces and the analysis of threat intelligence sources to identify evolving toolkits.

The dark web refers to a subset of the internet that is not indexed by standard search engines and requires specialized software, such as the Tor browser, to access. This part of the internet is intentionally hidden and designed to protect the anonymity and privacy of its users. It is often associated with illegal activities, such as drug trafficking, weapons sales, and the trade of stolen data. However, the dark web can also be used for legitimate purposes, such as anonymous communication and sharing information in countries with strict censorship laws. The dark web is a complex and often misunderstood network, and caution should be exercised when using it.

RESEARCH AND DEVELOPMENT

Organized cybercrime groups have become increasingly sophisticated and effective in conducting research and development operations to advance their malware and improve their cyberattacks. These groups use a variety of techniques and strategies, targeting both human and technology weaknesses, to stay ahead of law enforcement and security experts.

From a technology standpoint, organized cybercrime groups conduct extensive research to identify vulnerabilities in software and systems that they can exploit. This involves analyzing code, examining system architecture, and identifying weaknesses in security protocols. Once vulnerabilities are identified, cybercriminals develop custom approaches, malware, and tooling to exploit these weaknesses. These may be sold on underground marketplaces or be leveraged by threat actor groups loosely referred to as access brokers[190], allowing other cybercriminals to purchase access and pivot directly into the Intrusion Lifecycle.

But criminals do not just focus on vulnerable technology — they heavily rely on human weaknesses as well. For example, according to the 2023 Verizon Data Breach Investigations Report, *"74% of all breaches include the human element, with people being involved either via error, privilege misuse, use of stolen credentials or social engineering."* Cybercriminals use this information to develop social engineering attacks, which are designed to trick individuals into divulging sensitive information. These attacks are becoming increasingly sophisticated, with cybercriminals using machine learning and artificial intelligence to create convincing fake emails and websites. The fact that someone can create a

---

[190] "Initial Access Brokers: Fueling the Ransomware Threat," Nicole Sette, Keith Wojcieszek, and Laurie Iacono, Kroll.com, September 23, 2023, www.kroll.com/en/insights/publications/cyber/monitor/initial-access-brokers-fueling-ransomware-threat

completely grammatically correct email in a dozen different languages with simple text prompts and copy/paste, is fairly impressive considering how poorly some phishing emails were written just five or so years before the writing of this book.

Another way that organized cybercrime groups advance their malware is by reverse engineering security tools and antivirus software. By understanding how these tools work, cybercriminals can develop malware that can bypass them. This allows malware to remain undetected by security software, making it harder for security experts to identify and eliminate the threat. Just follow a few reverse engineers or malware engineers on social media for the inevitable screenshots of VirusTotal submissions showing zero detections by all major antivirus logos — it's an impressive feat to watch unfold in real time. Cybercriminals are constantly evolving their malware generation and coding capabilities to stay ahead of law enforcement and security experts. This involves testing malware in sandbox environments to identify, or more brazenly, waiting for Incident Response vendors to post their critical write-ups, identify the weaknesses for them, and then they patch them accordingly.

I remember attending a webinar years ago that reviewed a particular piece of malware and identified a weakness in the way in which the malware acquired data, encoded it, and wrote it to disk temporarily before it exfiltrated it. The webinar covered how to decode the staged data so that Incident Response teams could more easily identify the data at risk from the malware-staging activity. The webinar was posted publicly on the Incident Response firm's website, where anyone could register with an email address and join at a set date and time. Hundreds did. It was about four days later that the current campaign for that version of the malware inexplicably stopped and then about seventy-two hours later, a new campaign circulated. Upon inspection of the *"new"* version of the malware, the encoding/decoding technique unveiled in the webinar no longer worked. In fact, the malware even included references within the code thanking the webinar and the speaker by name.

This cycle of testing and refinement allows cybercriminals to stay ahead of the curve and continue to launch successful attacks. This has a significant impact on society, as cyberattacks can result in stolen personal and financial information, disrupted businesses, and even physical harm. It is therefore crucial that individuals and organizations remain vigilant and take steps to protect themselves against these threats.

Specific examples that I have experienced, investigated, and handled over the years have included the following:

- **The Carbanak Group** is a cybercriminal group known for conducting extensive research to identify weaknesses in banking systems and then using custom malware to steal millions of dollars from financial institutions around the world. The group also reverse-engineered ATM software to develop a tool that could dispense cash from ATMs without the need for a card or PIN.
- **The Lazarus Group**[191] is a North Korean-backed group known for conducting extensive research to identify vulnerabilities in financial systems and cryptocurrency exchanges. The group has used custom malware to steal millions of dollars from these systems and has also reverse-engineered security tools to develop malware that can bypass them.
- **The Emotet Trojan** is polymorphic malware known for its sophisticated social engineering delivery techniques designed to trick individuals into opening malicious attachments or clicking on links

---

[191] I dive deeper into the Lazarus Group in Chapter 6.

in phishing emails. The creators of Emotet were known to conduct extensive research to identify the best social engineering techniques to use and have even created a machine learning module to improve the effectiveness of their attacks. The malware contained well developed modules, which allowed for remote command and control access, stored browser credential theft, delivery of secondary malware (TrickBot was commonly observed), email thread acquisition and hijacking, pervasive persistence, and network discovery and propagation techniques.

- **The DarkSide Ransomware Group:** This group was one of the original organized crime groups known for using a double-extortion technique before it became popularized and largely used by nearly all ransomware groups at the time of this book being written. The technique involved not only encrypting a victim's files (delivery and execution of ransomware), but also exfiltration of sensitive data and then threatening to publish the data if the ransom was not paid. The encryption and request for payment for a decryptor was the primary focus of the attack due to potential for large payouts[192], but the double extortion portion of the attack came into play with the DarkSide group then pressuring the victim that if they did not pay, they would be further extorted with the threat of their data being posted for the world to see that the victim had experienced a network intrusion.

- **WannaCry** infected hundreds of thousands of computers in more than 150 countries in 2017 and integrated code that had been

---

[192] Further explored in Chapter 6 under "*Why Do They Do It?*"

developed and subsequently stolen from the U.S. National Security Agency (NSA).[193]

- **Operation Aurora** was a cyber espionage campaign that targeted Google and other companies in 2009. The attackers used spear-phishing emails to trick employees into clicking on a link that installed a remote access trojan. Once installed, the trojan allowed the attackers to steal intellectual property and other sensitive data. The attackers used a variety of techniques to evade detection, including using encrypted communications and creating custom malware that was difficult to analyze.

- The **BlackCat ransomware group**, also known as **ALPHV**, was identified in 2023 conducting malvertising campaigns to trick individuals into visiting counterfeit websites and download pages. These pages were cleverly designed to look like the official website of the WinSCP[194] file-transfer application for Windows, but they actually distribute malware-infected installers. Incident response and security analysts assessed that the BlackCat group was exploiting the popularity of the program to potentially infect the computers of system administrators, web admins, and IT professionals, thereby gaining initial access to valuable corporate networks. They noticed ad campaigns promoting the counterfeit pages on both Google and Bing search pages. In this particular situation, The Kroll Intrusion

---

[193] Literally the pinnacle example of what I explore further in Chapter 6, particularly under *"Studying APT Tactics and Techniques"*. Marcus Hutchins, aka *"MalwareTech"*, identified a kill switch web domain, registered it, and brought the spread of the malware to a halt. Fun fact, Hutchins is from Ilfracombe in Devon, historically known as Devonshire, a county in South West England, that is coastal with a variety of cliffs and beaches. I was named after Devonshire England.

[194] WinSCP, which stands for Windows Secure Copy, is a widely used free and open-source SFTP, FTP, S3, SCP client, and file manager that has SSH file transfer capabilities. As of the writing of this chapter, it was being downloaded approximately 400,000 times weekly on SourceForge.com alone.

Lifecycle™ Step 0 (External Victim Scouting) began when an unaware user searched for "*WinSCP Download*" on Bing or Google. The search results included malicious ads that were ranked above the safe WinSCP download sites. When users clicked on these ads, they were directed to websites that hosted tutorials about performing automated file transfers using WinSCP. These tutorial sites did not contain malicious content, likely to avoid detection by Google's anti-abuse crawlers. However, they redirected visitors to clones of the official WinSCP website, which featured a download button. These clone sites used domain names that were similar to the real winscp.net domain for the utility, such as winsccp[.]com. When researchers would click the download button, they received an ISO file containing **setup.exe** and **msi.dll**. The **setup.exe** file was the bait for the user to launch, and the **msi.dll** file was the malware dropper that was triggered by the executable. At the point of installation completion, a Cobalt Strike beacon would launch in the background of the victim's system and establish a command-and-control connection. At this point, The Kroll Intrusion Lifecycle™ models step by step from successful Step 1 (Initial Exploit) and continuing through Step 6 (Mission Execution).

INITIAL ACCESS BROKERS (IAB)

Cyber or initial access brokers are individuals or groups who specialize in buying and selling access to compromised computer systems, networks, and databases. These brokers operate in a highly illicit and underground markets, where they offer a range of services to cybercriminals, including access to sensitive data, stolen credentials, and compromised systems. I gave a talk about a year ago talking about *"Threats, Trends, and Tactics"* and one of the comments that I had at the time was that access brokering by criminal groups had become as much a part of ransomware economics as criminals outsourcing their ransom demand negotiations to call centers with scripts for operators to follow or organized crime groups bidding on dark web forums to purchase access to their next victim network.

One of the primary ways initial access brokers profit is by selling access to compromised systems or networks that they have gained access to through dark or deep net marketplaces. They then resell their achieved accesses to other cybercriminals, who leverage the access to continue **The Kroll Intrusion Lifecycle™** moving on from Stages 2 or 3 for a range of malicious activities, including data theft, cryptocurrency mining, ransomware attacks, and botnet deployment. Initial access brokers (IABs) are a growing threat to organizations. These actors specialize in gaining access to corporate networks and then selling that access to other threat actors, such as ransomware groups. I have reviewed timelines for investigations and assessed that sometimes the IAB to threat actor handoff can be as quick as hours from initial intrusion to handoff to pivot.

IABs often use stolen credentials or vulnerabilities to gain access to networks, and they can sell access for as little as a couple hundred U.S. dollars. There are many groups that also offer custom-built malware, designed to bypass specific security controls and exploit vulnerabilities in target systems. To counter the activities of IABs, professionals need to have a deep understanding of the underground cybercrime market and the tactics, techniques, and procedures (TTPs) used by these brokers. This requires ongoing monitoring of dark web marketplaces and analysis of threat intelligence sources to identify potential threats in combination with managed detection and response (MDR) monitoring enterprise connected or reachable endpoints.

CHAPTER 10 - INSIDER THREATS

Insider threats are a major concern in the world of cybersecurity, as they represent a significant risk to organizations' sensitive data and critical systems. Insider threats refer to individuals who have authorized access to an organization's systems and data, but leverage their assigned access to exceed authorized access and ethical boundaries. Insider threats can take many forms, including current and former employees, contractors, and business partners. These individuals often have privileged access to sensitive data and critical systems, making them a prime target for cybercriminals looking to exploit vulnerabilities. A 2021 survey conducted by Egress identified that 94% of organizations surveyed had experienced an insider data breach in the past year. The most common types of insider data breaches were

unintentional data leaks (42%), **malicious** data exfiltration (38%), and **data loss due** to employee termination (20%)[195].

Incident response plays a critical role in addressing insider threats by detecting, responding to, and mitigating the effects of a cyber incident. Incident response teams must be able to quickly identify the source of the attack and take appropriate measures to contain and mitigate the effects of the attack. One challenge of responding to insider threats is that they often involve authorized users who have legitimate access to an organization's systems and data. This makes it difficult to detect insider threats using traditional security controls, such as firewalls and intrusion detection systems. According to a report by the Cybersecurity & Infrastructure Security Agency (CISA), *"To combat the insider threat, organizations should consider a proactive and prevention-focused insider threat mitigation program. This approach can help an organization define specific insider threats unique to their environment, detect and identify those threats, assess their risk, and manage that risk before concerning behaviors manifest in an actual insider incident."*[196] This may include passive and active monitoring of network activity, implementing layered access controls, and providing awareness training programs for authorized users. By implementing a comprehensive insider threat program and IR plan, organizations can detect and respond to insider threats quickly and effectively, minimizing the impact of cyber incidents and protecting their critical assets.

What follows is an analysis of real-world insider threats.

---

[195] Egress Research. (2021, July 13). 94% of organizations have suffered insider data breaches, Egress research reveals. Business Wire. www.businesswire.com/news/home/20210713005123/en/94-Of-Organizations-Have-Suffered-Insider-Data-Breaches-Egress-Research-Reveals

[196] "Insider Threat Mitigation Guide", CISA, November 2020, www.cisa.gov/sites/default/files/2022-11/Insider%20Threat%20Mitigation%20Guide_Final_508.pdf

CHELSEA MANNING

Chelsea Manning was a U.S. Army soldier who leaked classified information to WikiLeaks in 2010 and was convicted in 2013 of violations of the Espionage Act and other offenses. Manning had authorized access to sensitive information and was found to have downloaded hundreds of thousands of classified documents, including military reports and diplomatic cables, onto a CD labeled "*Lady Gaga*." Manning provided the classified documents to WikiLeaks, which then published them. The documents revealed details about U.S. military and diplomatic operations around the world, including information about civilian casualties in Iraq and Afghanistan. Manning was an insider threat because of the abuse of the authorized position and access to sensitive information they were entrusted with and had taken steps to intentionally violate obligations and oath to protect classified information. Manning was originally sentenced to 35 years in prison, but President Barack Obama commuted the sentence in 2017.

EDWARD SNOWDEN

Edward Snowden is a former National Security Agency (NSA) contractor who became widely known for leaking classified information in 2013. Snowden worked for Booz Allen Hamilton as a systems administrator and had access to highly sensitive documents related to the NSA's surveillance programs. In 2013, he began leaking classified documents to journalists, revealing the extent of the NSA's surveillance activities, including its collection of metadata on millions of phone calls and internet communications. Snowden's actions were a breach of national security and as a result of a U.S. government investigation into the insider threat, he fled the United States and sought asylum in Russia, where, as of the writing of this chapter, he has remained since 2013[197]. From the perspective of the U.S. government, Snowden was an insider threat whose actions violated the Espionage Act. Snowden leveraged his authorized placement and access to view, acquire, and exfiltrate classified information in violation of his security clearance and his U.S. Government oath.

---

[197] In October 2020, Russia's government granted Snowden's request for permanent residency. By September 2022, Snowden had been granted citizenship by President Vladimir Putin and in December 2022, Snowden had sworn an oath of allegiance to Russia.

GALEN MARSH

Morgan Stanley, one of the largest financial services companies in the world, suffered a data breach that exposed the personal information of 350,000 clients. The breach was caused by an insider threat, a Morgan Stanley employee named Galen Marsh. Marsh worked in the company's wealth management division and had access to sensitive client data, including names, addresses, account numbers, and investment information. In January 2015, Marsh began transferring data from Morgan Stanley's systems to his personal computer, which he then used to access the data from home. Over the course of several months, Marsh downloaded sensitive data on hundreds of thousands of clients, including some of the firm's wealthiest clients. The breach was discovered in June 2015, when Marsh's home computer was seized by the FBI during a separate investigation. The FBI found the stolen data on Marsh's computer and alerted Morgan Stanley. The company moved to immediately suspend Marsh's access and his position while the company launched an internal investigation into the breach. The investigation found that Marsh had accessed the data without authorization and had violated numerous corporate InfoSec and IT-related policies regarding the handling of confidential client information. Marsh was ultimately terminated from his position and separated from the company. Morgan Stanley notified affected clients about the breach and offered free credit monitoring services. In December 2015, Marsh was charged with unauthorized access to a computer and identity theft. He later pleaded guilty to one count of exceeding authorized access to a computer and was sentenced to three years' probation and 300 hours of community service. Marsh was also ordered to pay $600,000 in restitution[198] to Morgan Stanley.

---

[198] Concept covered further in Chapter 4.

HAROLD T. MARTIN

Harold T. Martin was a contractor for the National Security Agency (NSA) who was arrested in 2016 on charges of stealing classified information. At the time, Martin was an employee of Booz Allen Hamilton, the same company that had employed Edward Snowden, and had worked for the NSA and other government agencies as a contractor for over a decade. In August 2016, he was arrested after FBI agents discovered that he had allegedly stolen a massive quantity of classified data from the NSA and stored it on his personal computer and in his home. The stolen information reportedly included highly sensitive documents, hacking tools, and other materials related to the NSA's operations, including information about Russian hacking attempts and the agency's efforts to track terrorists. At the time, the theft was considered one of the largest in U.S. history, with authorities estimating that Martin had stolen terabytes of data over a period of several years. Martin faced multiple charges, including theft of government property and the unauthorized removal and retention of classified materials. He was held in custody while awaiting trial, and in March 2019, he pleaded guilty to one count of willful retention of national defense information. In July 2021, he was sentenced to nine years in prison, followed by three years of supervised release.

JUN YING

In 2017, Equifax, one of the largest credit reporting agencies in the United States, suffered a massive data breach that exposed the personal information of over 143 million consumers. An Equifax employee named Jun Ying, who was an executive in Equifax's U.S. Information Solutions division, leveraged insider information regarding the discovery of a network intrusion. In August 2017, Equifax had discovered evidence of exploitation of an unpatched portion of its internet-facing systems. Equifax executives formed a response team to address the vulnerability and conduct an investigation into the extent of the unauthorized access. Around the same time, Ying exercised stock options and realized a profit of over $950,000. According to the U.S. Securities and Exchange Commission (SEC), Ying then began communicating with colleagues about a potential breach at Equifax and sold all of his Equifax shares before the breach was publicly disclosed. On September 7, 2017, Equifax publicly announced the data breach, which was one of the largest and most significant data breaches in history. The breach exposed sensitive information on nearly 40% of the population of the United States. In March 2018, the SEC charged Ying with insider trading and the selling of his Equifax shares based on nonpublic information about the data breach. Ying settled the charges and agreed to pay over $55,000 in disgorgement and civil penalties.

JACK TEIXEIRA

In April 2023, the Washington Post released an explosive article[199] titled *"The Discord Leaks"* and not even two days later, the FBI arrested Jack Teixeira, a 21-year-old member of the Massachusetts Air National Guard, identifying him as the source of classified document leaks detailing classified American and NATO plans which had been appearing on social media platforms. The leaked documents contained sensitive information intended for senior military and intelligence leaders and offered insights into a range of topics, including reports marked at Top Secret level about the whereabouts and movements of high-ranking political leaders, tactical updates on military forces and positions, and geopolitical analysis based upon sources and intelligence. They also contained intelligence on both allies and adversaries, including Iran and North Korea, as well as Britain, Canada, South Korea, and Israel.

According to various media sources, the breadth of the military and intelligence reports that were shared was allegedly extensive, offering a window into how deeply American intelligence had penetrated branches of the Russian military, showing that Egypt had planned to sell Russia tens of thousands of rockets, and suggesting that Russian mercenaries had approached Turkey to buy weapons to fight against Ukraine. The leaked documents were shared on a private server[200] on the chat app Discord and were obtained by a member of the group where the documents were shared.

---

[199] Harris, S.; Oakford, S. (2023, April 14). "Discord member details how documents leaked from closed chat group." The Washington Post. www.washingtonpost.com/national-security/2023/04/12/discord-leaked-documents

[200] Toler, A. (2023, April 9). "From Discord to 4chan: The Improbable Journey of a US Intelligence Leak." Bellingcat. www.bellingcat.com/news/2023/04/09/from-discord-to-4chan-the-improbable-journey-of-a-us-defence-leak

ANALYSIS OF INSIDER THREATS: A THREE-CATEGORY PERSPECTIVE

Insider threats are an increasingly critical issue for organizations worldwide. It becomes easier to understand and address these risks by examining these threats through the lens of three distinct types of insider threat actors: **Malicious** Insiders, **Negligent** Insiders, and **Accidental** Insiders.

MALICIOUS INSIDERS

These individuals have a clear intent to cause harm, with a motive often driven by personal grievances, financial gain, or political/ideological reasons. They consciously choose to act inappropriately and are fully aware of the negative consequences of their actions. Examples of malicious insider threats include several of the prior named individuals who focused on:

- Theft of intellectual property or sensitive data
- Sabotage of systems or infrastructure
- Espionage or sharing confidential information with external parties

An example of this type of Insider Threat lies in the story of the former staff member of the Discovery Bay Water Treatment Facility in California. Formally accused by a federal grand jury for deliberately trying to disrupt the facility's safety and protection systems, the individual, Rambler Gallo, aged 53, had been a full-time worker for a private company in Massachusetts that was contracted by Discovery Bay to manage the town's water treatment facility. He had served in the role of "*instrumentation and control tech*" from July 2016 to December 2020[201].

According to the indictment, filed June 27, 2023, Gallo had installed remote control software on both his employer's systems and his personal computer. This software had allowed him to oversee instrumentation readings and manage the facility's electromechanical processes. After resigning from his job in January 2021, Gallo had used his personal computer to remotely access the facility's network with harmful intentions[201].

---

[201] Cimpanu, C. (2023). Former employee charged for attacking water treatment plant. BleepingComputer. www.bleepingcomputer.com/news/security/former-employee-charged-for-attacking-water-treatment-plant

The U.S. Department of Justice reported that Gallo had remotely sent commands to the water treatment computers to remove crucial software tools that were responsible for monitoring water pressure, filtration, and chemical levels in the water. The motive behind Gallo's actions, which had put the health and safety of Discovery Bay's 15,000 residents at risk, remained unclear. At the time of this writing, the indictment charged Gallo with *"one count of transmitting a program, information, code, and command to cause damage to a protected computer,"* in violation of 18 U.S.C. §§ 1030(a)(5)(A) and (c)(4)(B)(i)[202].

---

[202] Dark Reading Staff. (2023). Tracy Resident Charged With Computer Attack On Discovery Bay Water Treatment Facility. www.darkreading.com/careers-and-people/tracy-resident-charged-with-computer-attack-on-discovery-bay-water-treatment-facility

NEGLIGENT INSIDERS

These actors fall in the middle of the spectrum, between malicious and accidental insiders. They are not intentionally seeking to cause harm, but their negligence or carelessness leads to security breaches or other adverse effects. Negligent insiders may not follow established protocols, are inadequately trained, or are unaware of the potential consequences of their actions. Examples of negligent insider threats include:

- Ignoring or circumventing security policies and procedures
- Falling for phishing scams or social engineering attacks
- Misusing or oversharing access privileges

A great example of negligent insiders was the 2020 takeover of nearly 150 Twitter accounts[203] in which internal systems were compromised by external threat actors through vishing (voice phishing[204]) techniques. Twitter provided some insights into the intrusion that took place, which led to the compromise of numerous high-profile accounts, including those of former President Barack Obama, presidential candidate Joe Biden, and Tesla CEO Elon Musk. In a series of posts on its support channel, Twitter confirmed that the threat actors had gained access to the company's internal systems, supporting the theory that the attack could not have been carried out without access to Twitter's own tools and employee privileges. Twitter assessed that the attack was a coordinated effort by individuals who successfully targeted some of its employees with access to internal systems and tools. The access was then leveraged to take control of high-profile accounts and tweet on their behalf. While Twitter did not provide specific details on the tools the attackers

---

[203] Statt, N. (2020). Twitter reveals that its own employee tools contributed to unprecedented hack. www.theverge.com/2020/7/15/21326656/twitter-hack-explanation-bitcoin-accounts-employee-tools
[204] Explored further in Chapter 11

accessed or how the attack was carried out, dark web discussions included screenshots of an internal company admin tool, allegedly leveraged to conduct the account takeovers. It was suggested that a combination of social engineering, vishing, and internally provided access allowed for the reset of account email accounts and recovered passwords. The threat actors leveraged their account takeovers to promote cryptocurrency scam, which resulted in private individuals sending nearly $120,000 worth of bitcoin to the digital wallet address listed in the tweets.

ACCIDENTAL INSIDERS

This category consists of individuals who inadvertently cause harm without any malicious intent or conscious decision to act inappropriately. Accidental insiders typically lack the knowledge, training, or understanding of security practices, which results in unintentional security breaches. Examples of accidental insider threats include:

- Accidental disclosure of sensitive information through email or other communication (e.g., emailing the wrong address, uploading files to a file share that is over exposed, sending information to the wrong contact, etc.
- Loss of physical devices containing sensitive data (e.g., laptops, smartphones, tablets, removable storage such as hard drives and thumb drives, etc.)
- Unintentional installation of malware or ransomware (e.g., downloading *"freeware"* or *"recommended software"* from websites maliciously designed to appear legitimate, but allow for delivery of malware or remote access capabilities through the software downloaded, etc.)

To effectively mitigate the risks associated with these three categories of insider threats, organizations should adopt a multi-faceted approach that includes:

- **Comprehensive employee training and education:** Ensure that employees receive regular training on security best practices, policies, and procedures, with special emphasis on the potential risks associated with insider threats and how to identify characteristics of them.

- **Access control and monitoring:** Implement strict access controls, limit overly broad access rights, and continuously monitor user activities to detect, alert on, and move to prevent unauthorized access, misuse of privileges, or other unauthorized behavior patterns.

- **Incident response and recovery plans:** Establish clear procedures for reporting, investigating, and resolving security incidents, as well as plans for recovering from a breach and minimizing its impact.

- **Fostering a culture of security:** Encourage open communication and collaboration across all levels of the organization, promoting a sense of shared responsibility for maintaining security and addressing insider threats.

A great example of an accidental insider-related investigation occurred first hand years ago in which a client retained my team's services to investigation the root cause of unauthorized access to their Amazon Web Services (AWS) services, specifically virtualized server instances and payment card infrastructure to include backend databases. During the investigation, I remember inquiring of the client where they maintained their development and production instances for their websites which led to a conversation around code control and storage. The client was emphatic that they did not leverage outside code repositories services and all of their code as maintained internally and securely. Part of our investigation centered around a review of the code and our team identified hard coded passwords and tokens that could be leveraged to access the same infrastructure in question. I guided my team to expand our search in order to *"trust but verify"* the client's statements that they did not leverage third party or external code storage services. What we found, with some searching, was large portions of the same code on GitHub in a publicly available and exposed, version controlled, git repo. The client was correct in that they themselves, through policy and acceptable practice, did not officially leverage GitHub. Unfortunately, our investigation found that one of their contractors did and would store code on GitHub for personal code version tracking. One of the times that they had chosen to synchronize their code to their own personal repository for version control, they uploaded all of the code they had been working on in the production (PROD) environment and that contained the hardcoded credentials. My team ultimately assessed that based upon the timeline of the commits, the limited logging available from GitHub.com, and the subsequent abuse and misuse of the acquired credentials, that the timeline and source of the code being publicly and inadvertently exposed, was the most likely explanation.

By considering the different types of insider threat actors and addressing their unique challenges, organizations can more effectively protect their assets and reduce the likelihood of a costly and damaging security incident.

CHAPTER 11 - VIOLENCE-AS-A-SERVICE

Violence as a Service (VaaS) is a disturbing and growing phenomenon in the world of cybercrime that involves the use of the internet and the virtual world to facilitate and orchestrate physical violence in the real world. This type of crime is relatively newer and has been made possible by the anonymity of the internet and the growing availability of cryptocurrencies that allow for untraceable payments[205]. The primary aim of VaaS is to provide a means for individuals to anonymously hire oghdfx to commit violent acts against specific targets. The perpetrators of these crimes are often hired through dark web marketplaces that offer a range of illegal services, including drug trafficking, arms dealing, and human trafficking. These marketplaces largely all exist within the dark web or deep net, beyond the search engine reach of the open, surface web internet (the internet most of the world's population interacts with). Anonymizing tools such as Tor are used to conceal the identity of their users and make it more difficult for governments, corporations, and law enforcement agencies to track back.

Additionally, as I worked on the research for this book, I identified a fair amount of content indicative of lone wolves who previously specialized in one form of criminal activity, selectively starting to expand (recklessly) into the VaaS space. For example, reports surfaced in late 2022 where actors who used to focus on SIM swapping, a crime relatively distanced from their victims, began offering violent services such as *"paying one another to fire guns into peoples' houses, throw bricks through their windows, firebomb buildings, or even advertise offers to rape specific people on their payers behalf..."*.[206] More of my research focused on and identified traditional criminals pivoting to the anonymity of the internet to push their agendas and further their real-world criminality.

---

[205] "Violence-as-a-Service: Brickings, Firebombings & Shootings for Hire", Brian Krebs, September 4, 2022, https://krebsonsecurity.com/2022/09/violence-as-a-service-brickings-firebombings-shootings-for-hire/

[206] "Firebombs and Shootings: The Rise of IRL Harassment and Violence as a Service", Joseph Cox, Motherboard/Vice, September 14, 2022, www.vice.com/en/article/3advxj/firebombings-shootings-as-a-service-telegram

The primary aim of VaaS is to provide a means for individuals to anonymously hire someone to commit violent acts against specific targets. In late 2022, 21-year-old Patrick McGovern-Allen was arrested by law enforcement for having allegedly fired eight shots into the walls and windows of a Pennsylvania home after having been contacted and paid online to commit the real-world violent act. This was after the same individual had been connected to postings on the Discord app claiming to have been involved in other violent acts ranging from random shootings to fire bombings – *"If you need anything done for $ lmk/ I did a shooting/ Molotov/ but can also do things for ur entertainment."* [207]

The perpetrators of these crimes can be contacted through social media apps such as discord and telegram but are often hired through dark web marketplaces that offer a range of illegal services, including drug trafficking, arms dealing, and human trafficking. These marketplaces largely all exist within the dark web or deep net, beyond the search engine reach of the open, surface web internet (the internet most of the world's population interacts with). Anonymizing tools such as Tor are used to conceal the identity of their users and make it more difficult for governments, corporations, and law enforcement agencies to track back.

What follows is an analysis of real-world Violence as a Service stories.

---

[207] Clark, D. (2022, October 20). Shootings and firebombs: Violence-for-hire a new threat online. NewsNation. www.newsnationnow.com/cybersecurity/shootings-and-firebombs-violence-for-hire-a-new-threat-online

MEXICAN DRUG CARTELS, US MILITARY & SOCIAL MEDIA RECRUITMENT

In 2013, Mexican drug cartels [208] were outed as being responsible for recruiting American soldiers via social media platforms to act as clandestine paid hitmen for purposes of operating within the United States offering assassination services to drug cartels. First Lieutenant Kevin Corley, who was serving in the military at Fort Carson, pled guilty to conspiring to commit murder in 2012 after he was arrested by federal agents in a Texas border town. In 2012, First Lieutenant Kevin Corley, who at the time was serving in the military at Fort Carson, pled guilty to conspiring to commit murder after he was arrested by US Federal agents in a Texas border town. Corley had offered to provide military-level tactics and weapons training to cartel members and assemble a team of *"assassins"* while supplying them with weapons stolen from the U.S. military base where he was stationed. He acquired and re-sold two AR-15 assault rifles to undercover agents, whom he believed to be members of the Los Zetas cartel and in addition, provided five flak vests as evidence of his capabilities and access to military gear. Additionally, he had agreed to carry out the assassination of a rival cartel member and acquire 20 kilograms of stolen cocaine, for which he had demanded $50,000 and five kilograms of cocaine for himself. Corley's accomplices included Sergeant Samuel Walker, his cousin Jerome, and Army Reserves member Shavar Davis, who had served with him in Afghanistan. Corley and Samuel Walker were sentenced to 15 and 10 years in prison, respectively.

---

[208] Hastings, D. (n.d.). "U.S. soldiers accepting cash, drugs for Mexican Drug Cartel Contract hits." New York Daily News. www.nydailynews.com/news/national/drug-cartels-mexico-hire-u-s-soldiers-assassins-article-1.1454851

Separately, and a few years earlier, Pfc. Michael Apodaca, who was on active duty at Fort Bliss at the time, was arrested, and ultimately sentenced to life in prison, for the 2009 murder of Jose Daniel Gonzalez-Galeana, a member of the Juarez Cartel in Mexico and an informant for the U.S. Immigration and Customs Enforcement agency[209]. The Juarez Cartel paid Apodaca $5,000 to eliminate the undercover informant near his residence in a peaceful, affluent district of El Paso, Texas, just a few houses down from the local police chief. Apodaca *"ran out of rounds"* carrying out the hit and later called into his cartel member contact to report *"I did it."* Ruben Rodriguez Dorado, an ICE informant who ordered the assassination, pled guilty to murder-for-hire charges and also received a sentence of life in prison. Ruben Rodriguez Dorado, an individual that unfortunately had been an informant for ICE at the time and operated as a double agent who ordered the assassination, pled guilty to murder-for-hire charges and also received a sentence of life in prison. The wheelman for Apodaca, Christopher Duran, was sentenced to 20 years.

---

[209] "Soldier accused of being hit man for cartel", CNN, August 12, 2009, http://www.cnn.com/2009/CRIME/08/11/texas.soldier.arrested/index.html

HITMEN, CRYPTO & LIVE STREAMING

In 2019, a 29-year-old white supremacist in New Zealand used social media to announce his plans to carry out a terrorist attack on a mosque. The man allegedly paid for his weapons and ammunition using cryptocurrency, and he live-streamed the attack on social media,[210] bridging a gap between the virtual and physical words in a heinous way. His attack resulted in the loss of 51 lives, and he was sentenced to life in prison.

Another example of VaaS was uncovered in 2019, when the FBI, and some of my former FBI colleagues, arrested an American male for using a dark web marketplace to hire a hitman to kill his wife. The man had paid the marketplace in Bitcoin and provided detailed instructions on how he wanted the murder to be carried out. The supposed hitman turned out to be an undercover law enforcement officer and the man was subsequently arrested and charged with attempted murder for hire.

---

[210] "New Zealand mosque shooter given life in prison for 'wicked' crimes", Praveen Menon, Reuters, August 26, 2020, www.reuters.com/article/us-newzealand-shooting/new-zealand-mosque-shooter-given-life-in-prison-for-wicked-crimes-idUSKBN25M2QF

EGREGOR ORGANIZED CRIME GROUP & TRIPLE EXTORTION

In October and November 2020, the Egregor ransomware group targeted Barnes & Noble, a major bookstore chain in the United States and demanded a ransom. When Barnes & Noble refused to pay, Egregor threatened to leak sensitive data that it had stolen from the company, including customer information and employee data. In addition to the data leak threat, Egregor engaged in a form of triple extortion by sending a ransom note to Barnes & Noble's executives, threatening to release more data and "*burn their reputation*" if the ransom was not paid. So, to recap, they (1) stole data and threatened to post the data, (2) threatened the victim's executives, and (3) encrypted internal systems which caused a business interruption and data disruption event.

> *Egregor, or more specifically "egregore," is a term that originates from the occult. It's derived from the Greek word "egregoroi," which means "Watchers." The term is used in the occult and in certain philosophical systems to refer to a type of collective consciousness or group mind that is created when individuals consciously come together for a common purpose, like a kind of collective psychic entity or thoughtform.*

DARK OVERLORD & THREATS AGAINST CHILDREN

The DarkOverlord, a notorious cybercriminal group, has been known to use particularly aggressive tactics. In 2017, they targeted a school district in Columbia Falls, Montana, and not only demanded a ransom, but also sent threatening messages to parents, suggesting *"potential violence against their children"* if their demands were not met. The hackers went so far as to send individual messages to Columbia Falls families, threatening to harm students by name[211]. This led to the closure of over 30 schools in the district for several days. The group had gained unauthorized access to the Columbia Falls school district server and stole a significant amount of personal information, including names, addresses, contact info, and medical data for past and present students.

---

[211] Tabish, D. (2017, October 5). In Columbia Falls, A Shaken School District Moves Forward from Cyber Threats. Flathead Beacon. https://flatheadbeacon.com/2017/10/05/columbia-falls-shaken-school-district-moves-forward-cyber-threats

BITCOIN, THE DARKWEB, & THE ACID ATTACK

In 2021, an unnamed man in Italy was arrested for using a dark web marketplace to attempt to hire someone to carry out an acid attack against his ex-girlfriend[212]. According to a statement released by Europol[213] at the time, the Italian citizen allegedly spent 10,000 Euros (equivalent to $11,885 at the time) to hire a hitman. The hitman's services were advertised on a dark web promoting assassinations, accessible via the Tor network. The Italian authorities reported that the man requested the hitman to *"disfigure the woman with acid and confine her to a wheelchair."* The payment for the service was made using Bitcoin. Europol was able to trace the Bitcoin payment back to a cryptocurrency service provider based in Italy. "*The Italian police then made contact with the identified Italian crypto service provider, who verified the information discovered during the investigation and provided the authorities with additional details about the suspect.*"

---

[212] "Man Arrested for Hiring Hitman on Dark Web to Attack Ex-Girlfriend", Michael Kan, PCMag, April 9, 2021, www.pcmag.com/news/man-arrested-for-hiring-hitman-on-dark-web-to-attack-ex-girlfriend

[213] Europol. (2023, June 30). Dark web hitman identified through crypto-analysis. www.europol.europa.eu/media-press/newsroom/news/dark-web-hitman-identified-through-crypto-analysis

SOCIAL MEDIA & "RECRUITING" FOR A SCHOOL MASS CASUALTY

In 2022, a teen allegedly posted an ad on an undisclosed social media platform in an attempt to recruit other students to join him in a shooting and bombing attack at Berkeley High School, in California. An undisclosed individual who found the posting reported the threat to law enforcement, and officers were able to obtain a subpoena to identify the IP address responsible for the posting and subsequently executed a search warrant at a residence of a teenager who was a student at the same high school. In law enforcement's press release, they noted that they *"discovered parts to explosives, assault rifles, several knives and electric items that could be used to create additional weapons"*[214]

---

[214] "Teen Tried to Recruit Others for Mass Shooting, Bombing Plot at Berkeley High School: Police", Terry McSweeney, June 1, 2022, NBC, www.nbcbayarea.com/news/local/teen-tried-to-recruit-others-for-mass-shooting-bombing-plot-at-berkeley-high-school-police/2907988

COCAINE, HEROIN & MILLIONS IN CRYPTOCURRENCY

In November 2021, Simon Barclay from England was arrested for running a large scale, illegal drug supply network that consisted of possession and distribution of cocaine and heroin. His activity came to light after his use of the dark web was identified by the Eastern Region Special Operations Unit (ERSOU)[215] who alerted West Yorkshire Police and the Yorkshire and Humber Regional Cyber Crime Unit.[216] Computers seized during the raid on his residence led detectives to the location of the drugs and cryptocurrency, worth more than £5.85 million at the time of his arrest. Simon was ultimately ordered to pay more than £4.9 million under the Proceeds of Crime Act and was sentenced to nine years in prison.[217]

---

[215] Eastern Region Special Operations Unit. About Us. https://ersou.police.uk/about-us.html
[216] "Drug dealer ordered to pay back dark web cryptocurrency millions", BBC, April 27, 2022, https:// www.bbc.com/news/uk-england-leeds-65416812
[217] BBC News. (15 June 2022). Leeds 'hitman' Darkweb trial: Italian man guilty of plot. www.bbc.com/news/uk-england-leeds-61809398

JOHN MUSBACH, MURDER-FOR-HIRE & CRYPTO

In 2023, a Camden County, New Jersey man by the name of John Musbach pled guilty to a murder-for-hire charge and admitted to using a website that promised to *"kill someone in exchange for a cryptocurrency payment"*[218]. By way of background, in the summer of 2015, Musbach had exchanged illicit photographs and videos with an underage victim. After his arrest on separate Child Exploitation Material-related charges in March 2016, Musbach attempted to obstruct justice and have the victim killed to prevent testimony against him. Musbach paid approximately 40 bitcoin, which equated to around $20,000 at the time, for the murder to take place[219]. However, when Musbach was asked for an additional $5,000 to execute the murder-for-hire plot, he eventually asked for his hit to be canceled and sought a refund of his $20,000. The indictment cited violation of Title 18, United States Code, Section 1958[220], also known as the "*Federal Murder-for-Hire Statute*" which makes it a federal crime to use interstate or foreign commerce facilities in the commission of murder-for-hire.

---

[218] Rice, N. (2023, February 3). N.J. man admits trying to hire hitman to kill teenager he sent explicit photos. Peoplemag. https://people.com/crime/man-who-sent-explicit-pics-to-teen-pleads-guilty-to-murder-for-hire-plot/

[219] U.S. Attorney's Office, District of New Jersey. (2023, February 2). Camden County Man Admits Hiring Hitman on Internet. U.S. Department of Justice. www.justice.gov/usao-nj/pr/camden-county-man-admits-hiring-hitman-internet

[220] United States District Court, District of New Jersey. (2023, February 2). United States of America v. John Michael Musbach. U.S. Department of Justice. www.justice.gov/d9/press-releases/attachments/2023/02/02/ musbach.indictment_0.pdf

SWATTING-AS-A-SERVICE (SAAS)

Swatting is a practice described by the FBI as "*a form of harassment to deceive an emergency service provider into sending a police and emergency service response team to another person's address due to the false reporting of a serious law enforcement emergency.*"[221] One type of swatting involved security researcher Brian Krebs, when a cybercriminal retaliated against Krebs' reportedly by shipping heroin to Krebs' home with the intention to "*tip*" law enforcement in time for them to discover and arrest the researcher. As Krebs described it, the criminal's plan was to "*spoof a call from one of my neighbors to the local police informing them that I was a druggie, that I had druggie friends coming in and out of my house all day long, and that I was even having drugs delivered to my home.*"[222]

Another example that took a tragic turn was when an argument between two online gamers resulted in the death of an innocent man completely unknown to them, Andrew Finch, whose address was randomly provided by one of the gamers after the other threatened to swat him.[223]

In April 2023, media reports surfaced about a service called Torswats, operating from a Telegram account, whose operator(s) offer various swatting services for a price, paid in cryptocurrency. For $75, Torswats stated they "*would close down a school*" and for $50, Torswats stated customers could buy

---

[221] "FBI Las Vegas Federal Fact Friday: The Dangers of Swatting," Sandra Breault, September 23, 2022, www.fbi.gov/contact-us/field-offices/lasvegas/news/press-releases/fbi-las-vegas-federal-fact-friday-the-dangers-of-swatting
[222] "Hacker Who Sent Me Heroin Faces Charges in U.S.", Brian Krebs, Krebs on Security, October 13, 2015, https://krebsonsecurity.com/2015/10/hacker-who-sent-me-heroin-faces-charges-in-u-s/
[223] "What is swatting? Unleashing armed police against your enemies," Josh Fruhlinger, CSO Online, November 25, 2020, www.csoonline.com/article/3573381/what-is-swatting-unleashing-armed-police-against-your-enemies.html

"*extreme swattings*," with a focus on causing law enforcement to respond to residences and cause chaos and panic with unsuspecting victims[224].

During my career in the FBI, I was attached to several investigations responding to individuals involved in this "*swatting*" practice, and almost always it was teenagers and young adults not thinking clearly about the repercussions of their actions. I recall one instance in which the Cyber squad I was attached to at the time was investigating and supporting local law enforcement on investigative leads to track down a suspected individual who had called in bomb threats to a string of schools in a particular region of the country. Where the individual eventually made an egregious mistake was in their assumption that they could not be found or caught due to their use of VPN services and voice anonymizers on their 911 phone calls, and they took a bet via a private forum that they could not get the FBI to specifically respond in one of the swatting incidents. When he called in a bomb threat to

---

[224] "A Computer Generated Swatting Service Is Causing Havoc Across America", Joseph Cox, Motherboard/Vice, April 13, 2023, www.vice.com/en/article/k7z8be/torswats-computer-generated-ai-voice-swatting

a local FBI office, the FBI officially got involved and within two weeks we had the subpoena and search warrant returns to identify the individual with specificity. We secured the search warrant for the home and executed. I still remember the moment when myself and another Special Agent were taking pictures of the search scene and inventorying equipment when we realized that the individual, at the time of our knock, announce, and warrant execution, was actually logged into a chat room, talking and planning his next swatting event and collecting payments for it.

Sometimes the evidence speaks for itself.

VOICE CLONING-AS-A-SERVICE (VCAAS)

While writing this book, I tried to think of what might be on the horizon for potential threats that may come to more light after this is published. One of the items that my research for this chapter led me to was the proliferation of voice deepfake technology, powered by artificial intelligence (AI), which has raised significant concerns within the realm of cybersecurity. While voice deepfakes offer intriguing possibilities for entertainment and personal use, they also pose substantial risks to organizations' data security, overall defense, and the ability to validate legitimate users.

With technological advancements, voice deepfakes have become astonishingly authentic, making it increasingly challenging to distinguish them from genuine voice recordings. Cybercriminals can generate convincing manipulated audio using minimal source material, thereby amplifying the potential for deception. Furthermore, the accessibility and affordability of

AI-powered tools have contributed to the widespread use of voice deepfakes, heightening concerns associated with this technology.[225]

This activity has grown to such an extent that the FBI issued a warning[226] in June 2022 documenting and calling out the increase in complaints. The FBI Internet Crime Complaint Center (IC3) issued a warning about the growing use of deepfakes and stolen personal data to apply for remote and work-from-home jobs. Deepfakes were being reported in context of manipulated videos, images, and recordings that convincingly misrepresented someone else's actions or words. The jobs targeted in the reported fraudulent applications often involved IT, computer programming, and software-related roles. The goal of the targeting was for threat actors to be provided access to sensitive data, including personal information of customers, financial data, and proprietary corporate information. The IC3 reported that it had received reports of voice spoofing and voice deepfakes being used during

> *The Internet Crime Complaint Center (IC3) is a division of the Federal Bureau of Investigation (FBI) that focuses on suspected Internet-facilitated criminal activity. It provides a convenient and easy-to-use reporting mechanism that alerts authorities of suspected criminal or civil violations. The center collects reports of Internet crime from the public and has received more than 7.3 million complaints since its inception (as of 2023).*

---

[225] The first reported instance of an artificial intelligence-generated voice deepfake used to commit fraud dates back to 2019, when a UK-based CEO, believing he was receiving instructions from his parent company's Germany-based chief executive, processed a $243,000 payment to ultimately an actor-controlled account. "Fraudsters Used AI to Mimic CEO's Voice in Unusual Cybercrime Case", Catherine Stupp, Wall Street Journal, August 30, 2019, www.wsj.com/articles/fraudsters-use-ai-to-mimic-ceos-voice-in-unusual-cybercrime-case-11567157402

[226] FBI Internet Crime Complaint Center. (2023, June 20). Deepfakes and Stolen PII Utilized to Apply for Remote Work Positions. www.ic3.gov/Media/Y2022/PSA220628

online job interviews, complete with auditory elements of the interviewee coughing or sneezing. The FBI also reported that it had received complaints about the use of stolen personal data to apply for remote positions.

Moving beyond AI and software tools though, my research for this part of the book also identified the growing availability of easy-to-use voice cloning platforms on the dark web. These platforms, some of which were free or cost as little as $5 per month at the time of this writing[227], were being leveraged to lower the entry barriers for cybercriminals. Threat intelligence teams at Kroll had been monitoring discussions among cybercriminals about being able to use these tools for impersonation, call-back scams, and voice phishing. Interestingly, some criminals were discussing their misuse and abuse of legitimate tools designed for audio book voiceovers, film and television dubbing, voice acting, and advertising to further their illicit purposes.

Voice deepfakes present multifaceted risks that encompass data protection, organizational security, and user verification. The following examples illustrate the potential dangers:

- **Exploiting Social Engineering Attacks:** Malicious actors leverage voice deepfake technology to execute sophisticated social engineering attacks, exploiting human vulnerabilities. By convincingly impersonating trusted individuals like company executives or customer support representatives, cybercriminals manipulate victims into divulging sensitive information or performing unauthorized actions. For instance, as explored in a report published by Recorded Future, *"I Have No Mouth and I Must*

---

[227] Infosecurity Magazine. (2023, June 21). Experts Warn of Voice Cloning-as-a-Service. www.infosecurity-magazine.com/news/ experts-warn-of-voice/

Do Crime"[228], an attacker could use a voice deepfake of a CEO to call an employee and demand the immediate transfer of funds to an external account. The deceptive authenticity of the deepfake could lead the employee into unwittingly facilitating a substantial financial loss for the organization.

- **Amplifying Phishing and Fraudulent Activities:** Voice deepfakes enhance phishing attacks, making them more persuasive and difficult to identify. Cybercriminals employ manipulated audio to replicate the voices of trusted individuals, thereby tricking victims into revealing confidential information or engaging in harmful actions. Consider a scenario where fraudsters use a voice deepfake to mimic a well-known bank representative in a phone call to a customer. The fraudster convinces the customer to disclose their account credentials, subsequently gaining unauthorized access and potentially perpetrating financial fraud.

- **Undermining Digital Evidence Integrity:** Voice deepfakes can undermine the credibility of audio evidence in legal proceedings, eroding trust in the justice system. By creating manipulated voice recordings that appear authentic, malicious actors introduce doubt into the veracity of the evidence presented. In a high-stakes scenario, similar to cases highlighted by the FBI, voice deepfakes could be used to fabricate incriminating audio evidence against an innocent individual. The authenticity of such deepfakes could cast doubt on the integrity of the evidence, potentially jeopardizing the outcome of legal proceedings.

---

[228] "I Have No Mouth, and I Must Do Crime", Recorded Future/Insikt Group, May 18, 2023, https://go.recordedfuture.com/hubfs/reports/cta-2023-0518.pdf

- **Challenging User Authentication:** Organizations that might rely on voice biometrics for user authentication could face challenges due to the rise of voice deepfakes. Cybersecurity teams will have to address the possibility of fraudsters bypassing voice-based authentication systems by employing manipulated recordings.

Effectively combating the risks associated with voice deepfakes would necessitate a comprehensive approach that combines advanced detection technologies, user education, and robust security practices.

CHAPTER 12 - DATA GOVERNANCE, RISK, AND COMPLIANCE (GRC) MEET IN #DFIR

When a cyber incident occurs, a three-part support system typically comes into play. Insurers often get the initial call, followed by legal counsel, and then Digital Forensics and Incident Response experts. With these three stakeholders in place, an organization can begin its remediation and recovery in a way that is legally sound and — hopefully — covered by their cyber insurance policy. While Digital Forensics examiners and incident responders may take many routes for the investigation, collaborating with the client's data governance, risk, and compliance (GRC) team may enable a faster response in certain circumstances, including an enhanced understanding of the incident[229] and an accelerated recovery.

For purposes of this chapter, I like this definition of data GRC: "...*a structured way to align IT with business goals while managing risks and meeting all industry and government regulations.*"[230] In many ways, knowing the GRC processes in place prior to an incident can provide an investigator with solid leads for how an incident played out. For example, what kind of data security controls were in force? They can provide leads for how an actor may have gained access, compromised user accounts, or moved through a network. Did the

---

[229] www.kroll.com/en/insights/publications/cyber/kroll-intrusion-lifecycle
[230] https://aws.amazon.com/what-is/grc/

organization account for and understand how operations intersected with data in the cloud and who is responsible for that data's security? Knowing this can help investigators with the access and lateral movement questions, as well as potentially data at risk. Sometimes, GRC efforts focus heavily on technology solutions, but neglect or postpone getting human team members up to speed on holistic data-related security strategies. In these cases, the incident responder needs to take time to gauge the *"big picture."*

Specifically, there are four key areas of GRC focus where incident responders can develop valuable digital forensic evidence and context in collaboration with internal GRC professionals:

1. Data Security Controls
2. Avoiding Blind Reliance on Cloud Service Providers
3. Investing in The Team
4. Collaboration with Legal Teams

DATA SECURITY CONTROLS

Discussion and knowledge of data security controls can help Digital Forensics examiners and incident responders understand what could have happened in the victim's environment. GRC teams can provide insight and investigative leads into where confidential data is held and what access rights were implemented prior to the incident.

For example, imagine a situation where fraudulent transactions are occurring due to a website payment card compromise, GRC teams can point to where records of accounts are, or should have been, kept. A subsequent investigation can expose problematic practices with how databases may have been managed or overall access was handled, or how some employees interacted with data, such as inappropriately saving data on personal computers. Issues like these, when combined with failures in cybersecurity best practices (think employees falling victim to phishing attacks), can lead to the creation of malware on the employee's computer and expose personally identifiable information (PII).

AVOIDING BLIND RELIANCE ON CLOUD SERVICE PROVIDERS

When cyber incident investigations cross over into cloud environments, the lines of responsibility may become hazier for some. Without appropriate GRC processes in place, forensic examination, remediation, and recovery can be hindered significantly. Log retention is critical when incidents involve the cloud. Much of an incident responder's digital forensic processes rely on access to log data over a significant period of time that can show cybercriminal activity and provide contextual detail on impacted systems and the required remediation.

If cloud providers are only retaining logs for 30 days, or worse, log retention isn't enabled by default, this can significantly impact the incident responder's visibility. It also potentially puts the organization at risk of violating data privacy laws, given the shared security model [231] that imposes security obligations on both parties. Clear and robust policies around cloud environments and an understanding of where responsibility lies will help safeguard that when digital forensic investigations take place[232].

---

[231] www.kroll.com/en/insights/publications/cyber/smb-guide-to-cloud-security
[232] www.kroll.com/en/insights/publications/cyber/guide-to-cloud-penetration-testing

INVESTING IN YOUR TEAM

Collaboration between the GRC and Digital Forensics team doesn't only provide clarity around the data access involved in an investigation. It also serves to build an organization's cyber resiliency and reduce the risk of non-compliance. This is seen most clearly when technologies or processes exist to address a data governance issue, but the team built around it hasn't received requisite or ongoing training. Whether it is due to a company's security mindset not evolving as a company grows, or a series of acquisitions and team turnover that have complicated processes and reduced retained knowledge, often the GRC processes which exist in theory are less apparent in practice.

Policies and procedures can be exposed as a *"paper exercise"* in the course of an Incident Response investigation, when digital forensic examiners are tracing data throughout the company. In the worst-case scenario, it is not just a lack of tick boxes, but actual infrastructure that is connected with insecure configurations, leaving web servers and database servers vulnerable to cyberattacks and interconnected with internal resources and networks. Without proper network segmentation inside the company, this situation is worsened as cybercriminals can move laterally to cause maximum damage. It is important that as part of the post-investigation recovery, the organization makes the investment to ensure someone has oversight and leads the effort to get these systems and processes in order. Doing so will benefit the company from both a cybersecurity and GRC perspective.

COLLABORATION WITH LEGAL TEAMS

Finally, knowing when to escalate a Digital Forensics investigation to an external legal support team[233] can be fundamental to handling an incident effectively and not exposing a company to further potential damage. While an investigation may have begun with a narrow scope, teamwork between GRC teams and digital forensic examiners can highlight when the data compromised represents a significant risk, which may require the investigation to continue under privilege. Legal teams experienced with advising on cybersecurity incidents are especially ready to hit the ground running, specifically external Cyber Privacy law firms and attorneys who regularly consult on data security incidents possessing near-real time knowledge and hands-on experience working in lockstep with Incident Response teams like mine. They typically have helped other clients navigate the many regulatory and reputational issues that arise in a cybersecurity incident as DFIR teams are concurrently working to stabilize the environment and deliver defensible findings regarding the incident.

---

[233] www.kroll.com/en/services/cyber-risk/incident-response-litigation-support/cyber-litigation-support

DIGITAL FORENSICS AND GRC TEAMS IN HARMONY

It may seem obvious that GRC teams and digital forensic examiners would have plenty of mutual interest, given their focus on understanding data flow and the processes and procedures that surround data, but they can be very much siloed within an organization. It is only when an investigation begins[234], such as in reaction to a cyber incident, that the synergies between teams become evident. Good collaboration across the two fields can also deliver longer-term, advantageous gains for both disciplines. From a cybersecurity perspective, sufficient resources and teams to implement the GRC policies will improve resiliency against cyberattacks. From a GRC perspective, among other advantages, data visibility and clear processes for handling logs will bring compliance issues to the surface and allow leaders to prioritize implementation before legal action ensues.

---

[234] www.kroll.com/en/services/cyber-risk/incident-response-litigation-support

CHAPTER 13 -
"EDR, MDR & XDR, OH MY!"

In the modern, complex world of cybersecurity, endpoint detection and response (EDR) has emerged as a vital tool in the arsenal of modern enterprise network defense. EDR and its variations — i.e., managed detection and response (MDR) and extended detection and response (XDR) — are all designed to monitor, detect, and allow for customizable response to potential threats and suspicious activities on endpoints, which include computers, servers, and other devices within a network. While all essentially work to protect the enterprise, let us take a look at how they differ.

ENDPOINT DETECTION AND RESPONSE (EDR)

A key feature of EDR is its ability to act similarly to an airplane's *"black box flight recorder"* in recording and capturing telemetry data. In the context of EDR, telemetry refers to the real-time data collected and transmitted by these products. This data provides a continuous stream of information about security events, process execution, and activities occurring on the endpoints within the operating system. It forms the backbone of threat detection and response strategies, enabling security and Incident Response teams like the ones I lead globally to be able to sift through the noise of a global enterprise of IT systems and narrow in on anomalous or suspicious events or incidents.

The richness of telemetry data that EDR products provide varies, and this can significantly impact the speed and effectiveness of threat detection and response. Therefore, understanding what constitutes EDR telemetry is crucial for executives. EDR telemetry encompasses several event categories that are critical for effective threat hunting and detection:

- **Process Execution:** Information about processes running on endpoints, such as process names, command-line arguments, and parent-child relationships.
- **File System Activity:** Details about file creation, modification, deletion, and other file system events[235].
- **Network Connections:** Information about network connections made by processes, including IP addresses, port numbers, protocols, and connection states.

---

[235] Covered in Chapter 3

- **Scheduled Tasks and Services:** Information about scheduled tasks and services running on endpoints, including task names, execution times, triggers, actions, and service status.
- **Registry Activity:** Data related to changes in the Windows Registry, such as the creation, modification, or deletion of registry keys and values.
- **System Configuration Changes:** Information about changes in system settings, security policies, and other configuration details.
- **User Account Activity:** Details covering user account activity, including logins, logouts, and other user-related events on monitored endpoints.

MANAGED DETECTION AND RESPONSE (MDR)

In the context of modern enterprise network defense, EDR plays a pivotal role. However, managing EDR can be complex and resource-intensive, which is where managed detection and response (MDR) comes into play. MDR is a managed cybersecurity service that enhances an organization's threat detection and response capabilities which is something Kroll Cyber provides. MDR's purpose is to provide real-time, 24/7 monitoring and Incident Response to potential cyberattacks, backed by a dedicated security team of experienced experts who understand situational context and The Kroll Intrusion Lifecycle™.

MDR offers several key benefits:

- **A Dedicated Security Team:** MDR provides a personalized service managed by certified, educated, and experienced experts who understand your specific network environment and organizational business risks.
- **24/7 Security Monitoring:** MDR ensures continuous monitoring for threats, enabling swift recognition of abnormal activity, events, and incidents, allowing for near-real time response to contain and eject maliciousness in the early stages of The Kroll Intrusion Lifecycle™.
- **Customizable Security Rules:** MDR allows for the application of an organization's security and operational policies, which can be updated to align with changing business needs and evolving threats.
- **Vulnerability & Attack Surface Scanning:** MDR can be leveraged as part of a robust vulnerability scanning and threat intelligence service to develop a prioritized list of evolving vulnerabilities, patch levels, and attack surface area.

- **Workflow Integration:** MDR ensures that event data, alerts, and incidents are properly prioritized and escalated so that issues can be remediated before they become a larger problem.

EXTENDED DETECTION AND RESPONSE (XDR)

Extended detection and response (XDR) is a cybersecurity technology that monitors and mitigates cybersecurity threats. XDR is not just another tool, but a collection and integration of several concepts into a single MDR solution. XDR works by allowing for the correlation of event data across various network points, resources, and appliances that cannot themselves be monitored by traditional EDR sensors. The components vary from vendor to vendor, but often focus on enriching EDR telemetry data with timeline data originating from logging sources, such as NetFlow, firewall, and VPN devices, in order to provide context to events and incidents appearing on endpoints and more immediate correlation with perimeter-to-endpoint connectivity.

> *NetFlow* was a network protocol originally developed by Cisco used for collecting and monitoring IP traffic information and has become an industry standard widely supported by various network devices and software solutions. NetFlow as a more generic term describes the collection of data which details network traffic, including details such as the source and destination IP addresses, the number of packets and bytes, and the start and end time of the traffic flows. The value of the data in Incident Response is being able to have more specificity around malicious traffic in and out of a network as well as volume of data flowing, especially egressing from the network (data being stolen or taken by an unauthorized threat actor).

Correlation of the data sources enriches visibility and context and can enhance timeline understanding of how events on traditional IT endpoints originated or came to be. It can also allow for easier identification and alignment with network edge vulnerabilities, such as remote code execution (RCE) or Common Vulnerabilities and Exposure (CVE) appearing in products that allow for **The Kroll Intrusion Lifecycle™** Stage 0 and Stage 1 steps to take hold.

Virtual private network (VPN) *appliances, just like firewalls, may generate and record logging of activities and traffic. The value of this data is in the details that it records, to include a user account's originating IP address; the VPN pool of IP addresses assigned to the user inside the network; start and end times of the connected user's session; amount of data transferred; and any errors encountered during the session. Some VPN services may also log details about the type of device and operating system used, as well as the VPN server location chosen by the user.*

*Most **firewalls** generate logging of activities and typically include details such as the source and destination IP addresses, source and destination ports, the date and time of the event, the action taken (whether the traffic was allowed or blocked), and the protocol used (TCP, UDP, ICMP, etc.). These logs provide a record of all network traffic that attempts to pass through the firewall, including both permitted and denied traffic.*

ABOUT THE AUTHOR

Toward the end of my senior year in high school, beginning to think forward to college, I remember discussing with my family what it was that I wanted to *actually* do with my future professional life. Up until this point, I had been working part time at a computer repair and design business, Agape Computers, and was considering starting my own business. Computers were "fun", but could they be more than just a hobby? Could I turn a hobby into a career?

I recall thinking through web design, information security, and related computer science paths — this was the mid to late 90s and the *"dot com"* boom was in full swing. I was building and selling web design services and what began as a hobby actually led to the formation of my first business, AEI Web Design. With my foot in the proverbial door of local businesses building and designing their websites, I began to gain experience as a small business owner. As my clientele base grew, I became their go-to for system and network design, which later led to custom-built computer and server solutions and starting my second business, AEI Computer Tech.

It was around this time in my life when one evening, my mother brought me a magazine with a corner-turned page and encouraged me to read an article on something that sounded exactly like what she thought I would be good at. My eyes landed on an article describing the future state of the developing field of Digital Forensics. A field of study that *"bridged the gap between Information Technology, law, and investigative fact finding"* — well now, that did sound interesting. Fast forward a few years, I completed my undergraduate degree in Information Technology & Digital Forensics and landed an Honors Internship Program opportunity with the Federal Bureau of Investigation's New Jersey Regional Computer Forensics Laboratory (NJRCFL). It was one of the most awe-inspiring and career-developing opportunities of my life up to that point. I was able to work alongside Forensic Examiners for the FBI, a blend of Task Force Officers from neighboring state, local, and other federal agencies, FBI Special Agents, and FBI Information Technology Specialists-Forensic Examiners (ITS-FE) — I was hooked. When that internship came to an end, I rotated back to my home state of Georgia and transitioned to the FBI's Atlanta Division Field Office working alongside Special Agents and Forensic Examiners, until I received a New Agent's class

date at the FBI Academy. A spark of interest fired years earlier continued through to the merger of a passion for technology with an investigative focus on *"figuring out the how."* Arriving at the FBI Academy in Quantico, Virginia, and walking the hallowed halls and the Academy grounds where thousands of Agents had walked before me was truly humbling and inspiring, and it set the course for my future professional and personal life in more ways than one.

LIFE AND PIVOTAL CURVEBALLS

Around week nine of the FBI New Agent's Academy, amidst dealing with legal tests, studying, learning proper firearm handling, arrest tactics, and everything else in between, I received a phone call that no son ever wants to receive. My life course was about to abruptly be altered. My mother had experienced a sudden heart attack and responding paramedics had rushed her to the hospital where she had slipped into a coma and was unresponsive.

Wait…What? What had just happened? Just hours before, I had read an email from her, checking in on me and giving me an update on what she and my father were planning to do that evening, and that weekend. I departed the Academy on a flight heading for Atlanta — numb and wondering what would be waiting for me when I landed. Arriving back at my family home, I found the house empty. Quiet. The lights were on, but the smiles, the laughter, and exclamation of *"You're home!"* all hauntingly missing. The liveliness of my mother that had filled the rooms with voice, laughter, and happiness my entire life up to just months before had been suddenly ripped out. On the kitchen counter, I found her teacup with the teabag still set, waiting for the water that never had a chance to be poured.

Three days later, with her family around her at the hospital, she was called to her Eternal Home. She never woke up from the coma. I was never able to say a final verbal goodbye, but she knew. She knew I had been set on a journey of which she was proud. Surreal moments like these

sear memories into our hearts and minds. They define us as human beings, and they impact the trajectory of our life's course. Perspectives gained from the experience of life's lessons, both personal and professional, are powerful teachers if we allow ourselves to learn, to aspire, and to channel the grit into determination and focus.

Looking back, one of the fondest memories of my younger life is receiving and opening when I received and opened the Conditional Letter of Appointment to become a Special Agent for the FBI with my mother there to experience that moment — me in her office, reading the letter aloud, half wondering if the letter was simply a formality and only thanking me for applying, but perhaps would mention further down the page that I had not been accepted. Profound pride was shared that day. Now, sitting at my desk in my office, writing this book all these years later, I remember the incredible feeling of fulfillment standing on the stage of the FBI Academy grounds, surrounded by family and classmates, graduating the FBI Academy as a Special Agent – looking out at the crowd, but eyeing one chair empty next to my father.

Out of the Academy, I was assigned to the FBI's Charlotte Division (North Carolina), and embarked on a defining journey navigating criminal, terrorism, counterintelligence, cyber, and digital forensic investigations. Years in, I applied for and was accepted into the FBI's Computer Analysis Response Team (CART) as a Special Agent/Forensic Examiner. Over the course of my career with the FBI, I had the privilege and opportunities to expand my knowledge of forensics, network intrusions, and Incident Response, culminating with my successful completion of the FBI's Senior Digital Forensic Sciences Forensic Examiner certification program, one of the few FBI Special Agent/Senior Forensic Examiners in the history of the FBI's CART program at that time. Later in my career, I was able to return to the FBI Academy grounds, Quantico, Virginia, where I took an office as a Supervisory Special Agent (SSA) specifically at Operational Technology Division. My responsibilities included oversight and coordination of Digital Forensics-related field operations across the United States and internationally where FBI assets were involved in responding to and investigating domestic terrorism matters, mass shooting incidents, large-scale electronic evidence collections, intrusion/Incident Response events, and multi-agency investigations.

I was responsible, in part, for the program providing oversight, budgets and guidance for approximately 500 Forensic Examiners (e.g., Special Agents, Information Technology Specialists, and Task Force Officers), their management, and Senior Executive Staff (SES), including coordination, logistics, and technical support for Forensic Examiners deployed both domestically and internationally in support of Digital Forensics and Incident Response (DFIR) missions. I collaborated on the development of a number of widely used forensic tools and was the course material revision architect and co-author for the FBI's CART Tech Certification program and Digital Evidence Extraction Technician (DExT) training curriculums. I was involved in the implementation and organization of the FBI Field Instructor Program

(FiP) as well as the implementation and management of automated Digital Forensics classroom grading systems. I taught several Digital Forensics classes while I was at headquarters, and I estimate I taught educating more than 400 Agents, Task Force Officers, consultants, Computer Scientists, Intelligence Analysts, and private sector students during my time there.

ABOUTDFIR.COM & GIVING BACK

It was during this time that I started AboutDFIR.com, originally as a side project in a spreadsheet. After I arrived at Kroll, I spent time to mature the project into a full blown, standalone website to give back to the community, and it has become one of the internet's leading Digital Forensics and Incident Response compendiums of definitive knowledge about training, education, tooling, artifacts, jobs, and daily tech news, as well as myriad other related information and original content.

As my professional career has evolved, I have experienced a range of opportunities including:

- Guest speaker at SANS DFIR Summits, once on *"Microsoft 365 Forensics and Incident Response"* [236] and separately on *"Navigating Investigations of Unconventional Data Sources"*
- Awarded Digital Forensic Investigator of the Year
- Serve as a member of the Cybercrime Advisory board for the University of Florida, Department of Criminology, Graduate program – Master of Science in Cybercrime
- Spoken on NPR's Planet Money show, Lee Reiber's Forensic Happy Hour, as well as a range of podcasts including The Cyber Crime Lab, Sayata Cyber Insurance, LimaCharlie and others
- Been published in PenTest Magazine, Enterprise Security Magazine, GRC Outlook Magazine, Security Magazine, and others

---

[236] "A Planned Methodology for Forensically Sound Incident Response in Microsoft's Office 365 Cloud Environment", SANS DFIR Summit 2018, www.sans.org/presentations/a-planned-methodology-for-forensically-sound-incident-response-in-microsofts-office-365-cloud-environment

- Delivered keynote and panel talks at a range of conferences over the years, to include the 2022 and 2023 HTCIA International Conference and Expos and numerous NetDiligence and IAPP (International Association of Privacy Professionals)
- My forensic examinations, findings, and investigations have supported and resulted in forensic and expert digital evidence testimony in both federal and state courts
- Presented to executives and boards of directors during the Annual Association for Computer Operations Management (AFCOM)
- Served as a representative of the United States government to foreign delegations to include Belgian Federal Police, New South Wales and others, and while with Kroll to the Ukrainian Cyber Command delegation and others
- Presented on *"Cyber Threats, Trends and Tactics"* to the Illinois House of Representatives as well as various other government entities, bodies, and elected officials over the years

Made in the USA
Las Vegas, NV
22 September 2023